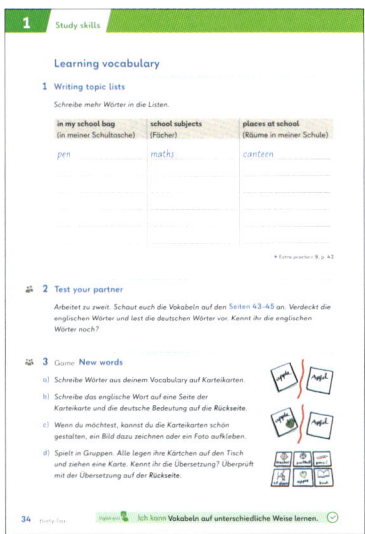

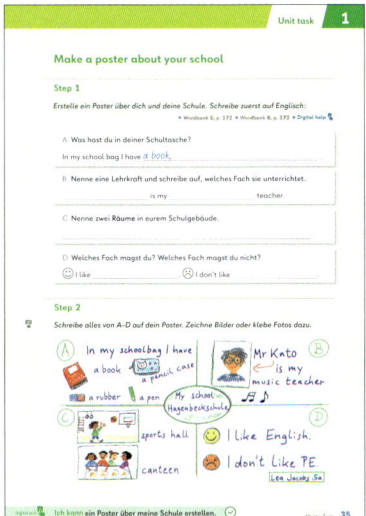

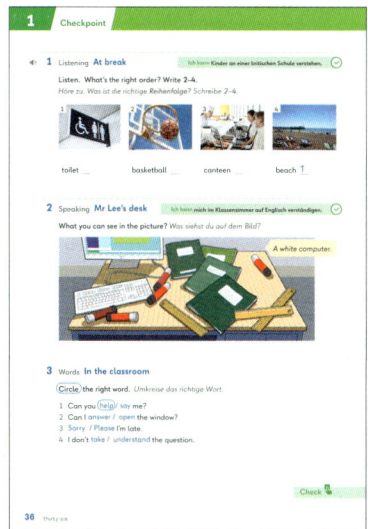

Study skills

Hier übst du wichtige Lerntechniken.

Unit task

In der *Unit task* erstellst du ein größeres Produkt, z.B. eine Präsentation.

Checkpoint

Hier überprüfst du, wie gut du gelernt hast.

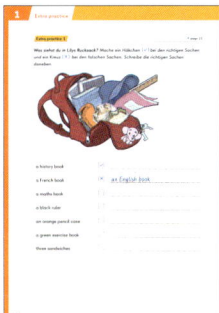

Extra practice

Am Ende jeder Unit findest du noch mehr Übungen.

Vokabelliste

Am Ende jeder Unit gibt es eine Liste mit den neuen Vokabeln. Hier kannst du nach Wörtern suchen und sie üben. Blaue Wörter kennst du aus der Grundschule.

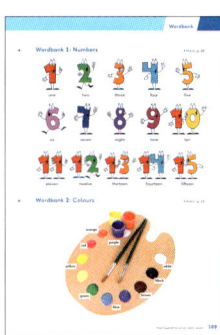

Wordbanks

Du hast neue Themen kennengelernt. Nach den Units findest du die Wörter dazu.

lighthouse 1

Lern- und Arbeitsheft für Lernende mit erhöhtem Förderbedarf
Lehrkräftefassung

Im Auftrag des Verlages herausgegeben von
Martin Bastkowski, Schellerten; Sonja Mahne, Basel;
Ulrike Rath, Aachen; Berit Schaarschmidt, Aschaffenburg

Erarbeitet von
Rebecca Robb Benne, Kopenhagen; Zoe Thorne, Haywards Heath
sowie Chris Maxwell, Berlin; Jennifer O'Hagan, Bristol (*Checkpoints*)

In Zusammenarbeit mit der Englischredaktion
Klaus Unger (Projektleitung), Sandhya Gupta, Chris Maxwell,
Karin Wedepohl, sowie Georg Raspe, Düsseldorf (Vocabulary)

Beratende Mitwirkung
Tina Göhlich, Hamburg; Stella Halank, Berlin; Lina Hein, Wuppertal;
Christina McCrum, Köln; Ulrike Plänker, Sprockhövel

Lizenzmanagement
Silke Kirchhoff

Illustrationen
Harald Ardeias, Schelkingen; Karen Donnelly, Brighton;
Irina Zinner, Hamburg; Josephine Bienert-Köhler, Berlin

Fotos
Anja Poehlmann, Brighton
Für die freundliche Unterstützung danken wir der
Varndean School, Brighton

Umschlaggestaltung: Rosendahl, Berlin

Layoutkonzept: Klein & Halm, Berlin

Layout und technische Umsetzung
Reemers Publishing Services GmbH; Straive

www.cornelsen.de

Die Webseiten Dritter, deren Internetadressen in diesem
Lehrwerk angegeben sind, wurden vor Drucklegung sorgfältig
geprüft. Der Verlag übernimmt keine Gewähr für die Aktualität
und den Inhalt dieser Seiten oder solcher, die mit ihnen verlinkt
sind.

Soweit in diesem Lehrwerk Personen fotografisch abgebildet sind
und ihnen von der Redaktion fiktive Namen, Berufe, Dialoge und
Ähnliches zugeordnet oder diese Personen in bestimmte Kontexte
gesetzt werden, dienen diese Zuordnungen und Darstellungen
ausschließlich der Veranschaulichung und dem besseren
Verständnis des Buchinhaltes.

Dieses Werk berücksichtigt die Regeln der reformierten Rechtschreibung und Zeichensetzung.

1. Auflage, 2. Druck 2023

Alle Drucke dieser Auflage sind inhaltlich unverändert und können
im Unterricht nebeneinander verwendet werden.

*Die **Cornelsen Lernen App** ist eine fakultative Ergänzung zu
Lighthouse, die die inhaltliche Arbeit begleitet und unterstützt.*

© 2022 Cornelsen Verlag GmbH, Berlin

ISBN 9783060358533 (Ausgabe für Lernende)
ISBN 9783060345465 (Ausgabe für Lehrkräfte)

Druck: AZ Druck und Datentechnik GmbH, Kempten

PEFC-zertifiziert
Dieses Produkt
stammt aus
nachhaltig
bewirtschafteten
Wäldern und
kontrollierten Quellen
PEFC/04-31-2260   www.pefc.de

lighthouse 1

Lern- und Arbeitsheft

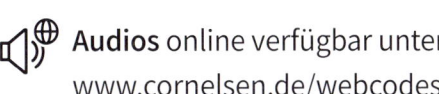 **Audios** online verfügbar unter
www.cornelsen.de/webcodes **Code:** bawehu

 Dein Arbeitsheft findest du auch in der **Cornelsen Lernen App**.

Siehst du eines dieser Symbole in deinem Arbeitsheft, findest du in der App …

 alle **Audios**

 alle **Videos** und **Erklärfilme**

 Hilfen und **Lösungen** zu ausgewählten Aufgaben

Unit 0 **Hello!**

Wenn du die Seiten bearbeitet hast, setze ein Häkchen in die Box.

Unit 1 **My new school**

Wenn du die Seiten bearbeitet hast, setze ein Häkchen in die Box.

Seite

My new school	Ich kann Kinder in einer britischen Schule verstehen. Hello. I'm Noah. I'm 11. My favourite hobby is taking photos.		18–19
Topic 1	Ich kann mich im Klassenzimmer auf Englisch verständigen. What page is it? I don't understand.		20–23
Topic 2	Ich kann meinen Stundenplan auf Englisch schreiben.		24–27
Topic 3	Ich kann meine Schule beschreiben. My favourite place in school is the art room. My school is great. I'm in class 7B. My class teacher is Mr Lee.		28–29
Story	Ich kann eine Geschichte über eine Freundschaft verstehen.		30–32
Study skills	Ich kann Vokabeln auf unterschiedliche Weise lernen.		34
Unit task	Ich kann ein Poster über meine Schule erstellen.		35

Unit 2 **My family and home**

Wenn du die Seiten bearbeitet hast, setze ein Häkchen in die Box.

My dream room

There's a big red sofa. There's a black cat on my bed. There are three computers. There are a lot of comics.

Unit 3 **My day**

Wenn du die Seiten bearbeitet hast, setze ein Häkchen in die Box.

Unit 4 **Where I live**

Wenn du die Seiten bearbeitet hast, setze ein Häkchen in die Box.

Seite

Where I live	**Ich kann Informationen über Brighton verstehen.** This is a good place for a picnic. You can go skateboarding here.		110–111 ☐
Topic 1	**Ich kann meinen Wohnort beschreiben.** I live in a big city. I don't like my neighbourhood.		112–115 ☐
Topic 2	**Ich kann über meine Stadt sprechen.** Does your town have a hospital? Yes, it does.		116–119 ☐
Topic 3	**Ich kann über Sehenswürdigkeiten und das Wetter sprechen.** It's sunny today. Where do you go when it's rainy?		120–121 ☐
Story	**Ich kann eine Geschichte lesen und verstehen.**		122–124 ☐
Study skills	**Ich kann eine kurze Präsentation vorbereiten.** This presentation is about my favourite place. Thank you for listening.		126 ☐
Unit task	**Ich kann eine kurze Präsentation halten.**		127 ☐

Unit 5 Enjoy!

Wenn du die Seiten bearbeitet hast, setze ein Häkchen in die Box.

Hello!
Nice to meet you

I'm Scout.
I'm a seagull.
I'm hungry!

Don't feed the seagulls.

1 Hello, Scout

Schau dir die Seiten 10–11 an. Richtig (✓) oder falsch (✗)?

1 Scout is a seagull. ☑   2 Scout is from Hove. ☒   3 Scout is six years old. ☑

2 What about you?

1.1
a) **Look at picture 4. Listen and practise.** *Schau dir Bild 4 an. Höre zu und übe.*

b) **Now ask and answer about you.** *Nun befragt euch gegenseitig.*

▶ **Numbers, p. 168**   ▶ **Wordbank 1, p. 169**

4

Hello!
I'm *Scout* the *seagull*.
What's your name?

Hi! I'm *Leo*.

I'm *six* years old.
How old are you?

I'm *ten*.

I'm from *Brighton*.
Where are you from?

I'm from *Hove*.

I like *sandwiches*.
What about you?

I like *football*.

5

6

You're clever!
Thanks!

👥 3 Hello, class

Walk around Talk to a partner. *Sprich mit einer Partnerin oder einem Partner.*

Hello. I'm …
What's your name?

Hi! I'm ….
I'm … years old.

I'm from …
Where are you from?

I'm from …
I like …
What about you?

Goodbye, holidays!

---

1 In the picture

1.2

a) Look at the picture. Listen, find and point.

Schau dir das Bild an. Höre zu, finde und zeige im Bild.

▶ Wordbank 2, p. 169

b) *Schau dir noch einmal das Bild an. Finde, zeige und sage, was du siehst.*

> Scout the seagull • Leo's mum • a ball • a boy •
> a girl • three things to eat • three animals

> Here's Scout.

> And here's Leo's mum.

> I can see a dog / …

c) *Schau dir das große Bild für 30 Sekunden an. Schließe dein Buch. Woran erinnerst du dich?*

> I remember Scout and a dog.

> I remember Scout.

> I remember Scout and a dog and a …

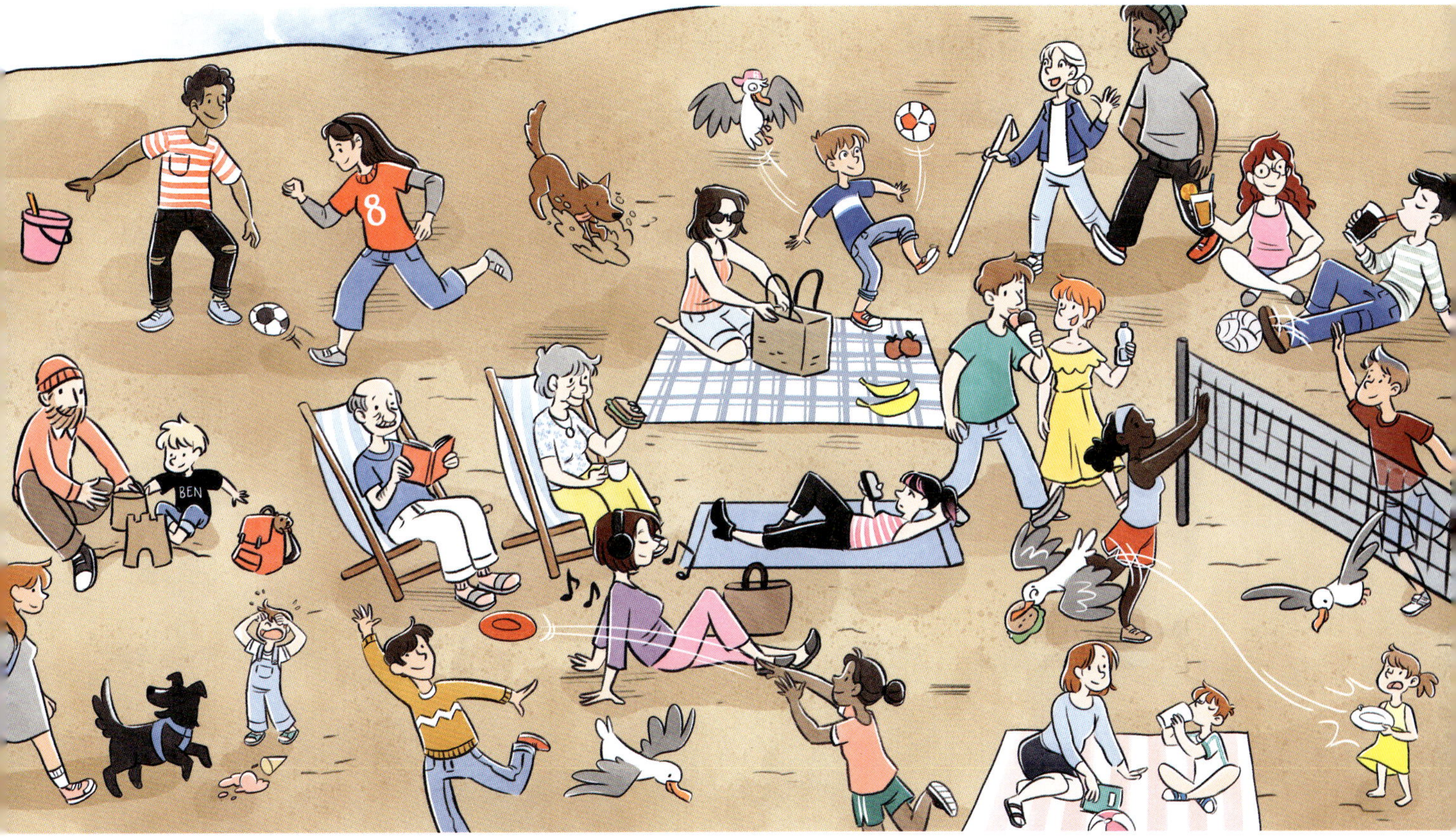

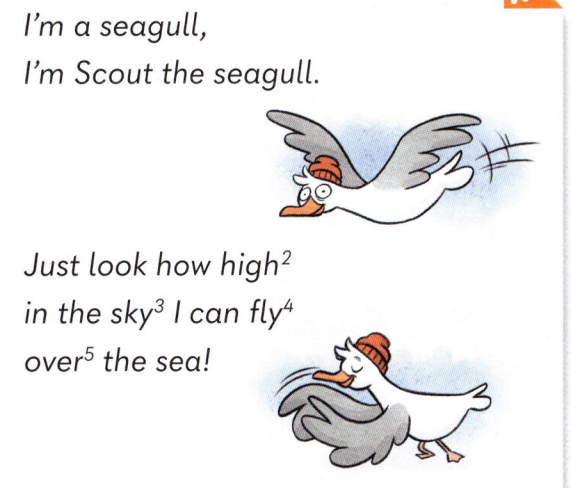

2 Song **Scout's song**

1.3

Listen to the song. Then listen again and sing.

Höre dir das Lied an. Dann höre noch einmal zu und singe mit.

Hi, hello,
nice to meet you today.

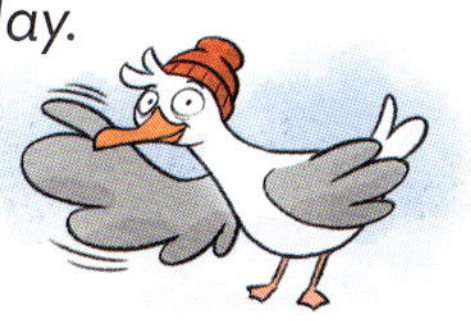

How are you?
I'm fine, I'm OK.

I live here in Brighton,
right by the sea[1]*.*

"Look out! It's Scout!"

I'm a seagull,
I'm Scout the seagull.

Just look how high[2]
in the sky[3] *I can fly*[4]
over[5] *the sea!*

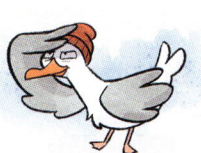

[1] **right by the sea** *direkt am Meer* [2] **high** *hoch* [3] **sky** *Himmel* [4] **fly** *fliegen* [5] **over** *über*

ital quiz **Ich kann über ein Bild sprechen.**

About me

1 My favourite animal

a) What animal is it? Write the correct numbers 1–8.

Welches Tier ist es? Schreibe die richtigen Zahlen 1–8.

__1__ a horse   __6__ a cat   __3__ a parrot

__2__ a dog   __5__ a lion   __7__ a snake

__8__ an elephant   __4__ a monkey

 1
 2
 3
 4
 5
 6
 7
 8

b) Listen and tick (✓) the animals you hear.

Höre zu und hake (✓) die Tiere ab, die du hörst.

1 monkey ✓   2 cat ☐   3 parrot ✓

4 dog ☐   5 elephant ✓   6 horse ✓

7 lion ✓   8 snake ✓

c) Mime, draw or make an animal noise. Your partner says the animal. *Stelle ein Tier pantomimisch dar, male es oder mache ein Tiergeräusch. Deine Partnerin oder dein Partner nennt das Tier.*

It's a dog!

▶ Wordbank 3, p. 170

d) Game *Stellt euch in einem Kreis auf. Ein Kind sagt sein Lieblingstier. Alle Kinder mit demselben Lieblingstier tauschen die Plätze.*

My favourite animal is a fish.

2 My favourite hobbies

a) Scout's hobbies: Write the words under the right pictures. *Schreibe die Wörter unter die passenden Bilder.*

> drawing • ~~listening to music~~ • swimming • taking photos

listening to music

drawing

swimming

taking photos

b) Double circle *Sprecht mit eurem Gegenüber. Dann geht ein Kreis einen Schritt weiter, damit jede/jeder ein neues Gegenüber bekommt.*

> My favourite sport is …
> What about you?

> 🙂 I like / I love …

> My favourite hobby is …
> What about you?

> 🙁 I don't like …

▶ Wordbank 4, p. 171

3 My favourite things

🔊 1.5

a) Look at the picture. Listen and repeat.
Schau dir das Bild an. Höre zu und wiederhole.

b) Find five things in the picture. Write the numbers 1–5 in the picture.
Finde fünf Dinge im Bild und nummeriere sie 1–5.

1. It's small and black.
2. It's big and blue.
3. It's small and gold.
4. It's big and silver.
5. It's red.

4 Song **My favourites**

Listen and sing.
Höre zu und singe.

What's your favourite animal?
My favourite animal's a kangaroo[1].
What's your favourite colour[2]?
My favourite colour is blue. What about you?

What's your favourite hobby?
Dancing[3] is my favourite thing to do[4].
What's your favourite sport?
I like swimming too[5]. What about you?

5 Scout's top five

Match. *Ordne zu.*

1 My favourite hobby is	swimming.
2 My favourite colour is	orange.
3 My favourite sport is	a fish.
4 My favourite thing is my	eating.
5 My favourite animal is	hat.

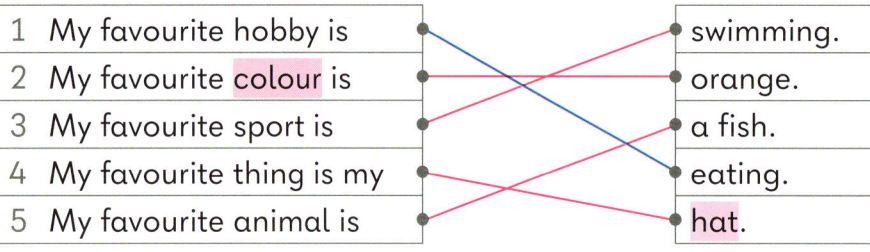

6 **My top five**

a) **Write your top five.** *Schreibe deine Top Fünf auf.*

1 My favourite animal is *(a horse)* .

2 My favourite colour is *(blue)* .

3 My favourite sport is *(swimming)* .

4 My favourite thing is my *(ball)* .

5 My favourite hobby is *(listening to music)* .

b) **Walk around Ask and answer questions.** *Stellt Fragen und beantwortet sie.*

What is your favourite ...?   *My favourite ... is ...*

---

[1] **kangaroo** *Känguru*   [2] **colour** *Farbe*   [3] **dancing** *das Tanzen*   [4] **do** *tun*   [5] **too** *auch*

Digital quiz 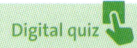   **Ich kann** sagen, was ich (am liebsten) mag.

Ready for school

1 Listen, please!

1.7 a) Listen. Point to the right pictures. *Höre zu. Zeige auf die richtigen Bilder.*

Listen.

Stand up.

Sit down.

Open your books.

Put your hand up.

Hello everybody!

1.8 b) Listen. Do the actions. *Höre zu. Führe die Aktionen aus.*

2 Song **The school song**

1.9 a) Listen. In what order do the actions come up in the song? Write 1–5. *Höre zu. In welcher Reihenfolge kommen die Aktionen im Lied vor? Schreibe 1–5.*

 1
 3
 2
  5
 4

b) Listen again, act and sing. *Höre noch einmal zu, stelle das Lied dar und singe.*

3 Where's Scout?

On what page of this book can you find these pictures of Scout? Write the page number. *Auf welchen Seiten in diesem Buch findest du diese Bilder von Scout? Schreibe die Seitenzahlen auf.*

S. 9/143

S. 126/184

S. 72

S. 27

S. 9/156

ital quiz **Ich kann** verstehen, was im Klassenzimmer gesagt wird.

Unit 1
My new school

1
1 **I'm** Sunita Chandra.
2 **I'm** (11) / 12.
3 **My favourite hobby is**
   drawing / (coding[1]).
4 **My favourite sport is**
   basketball / (yoga).

2
1 **I'm** Noah Williams.
2 **I'm** (11) / 12.
3 **My favourite hobby is**
   (taking photos) / listening to music.
4 **My favourite sport is**
   basketball / (walking[2]).

1 Listening **Four students at Varndean School**

a) Before you listen **What's Scout saying? Match.** *Was sagt Scout? Ordne zu.*

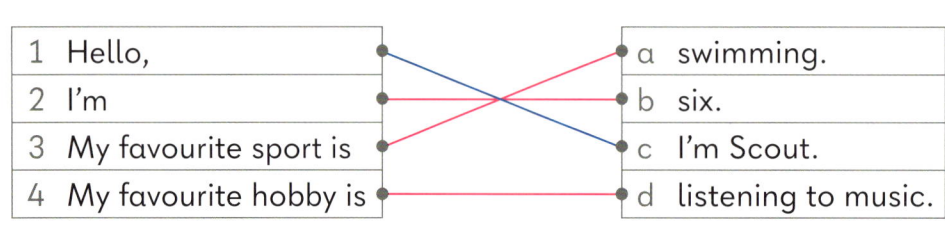

1 Hello,	a swimming.
2 I'm	b six.
3 My favourite sport is	c I'm Scout.
4 My favourite hobby is	d listening to music.

🔊 b) *Höre zu. Umkreise die richtigen Wörter unter den Fotos 1–4.*
1.10

[1] **coding** *Kodieren, Programmieren*   [2] **walking** *(zu Fuß) gehen, wandern*

Nach dieser Unit kann ich ...

○ mich im Klassenzimmer
   auf Englisch verständigen
○ meinen Stundenplan schreiben
○ meine Schule beschreiben
○ Vokabeln auf verschiedene Arten üben

Unit task

○ ein Poster über meine Schule anfertigen

3

1 **I'm** Zane Adebayo.
2 **I'm** 10 / (11).
3 **My favourite hobby is**
   (cooking[1])/ listening to music.
4 **My favourite sport is**
   (swimming)/ yoga.

4

1 **I'm** Lily Hall.
2 **I'm** (11)/ 12.
3 **My favourite hobby is**
   (drawing)/ listening to music.
4 **My favourite sport is**
   (parkour)/ football.

c) **Write about you.** *Schreibe über dich.*

1 *I'm* _____ .

2 *I'm* _____ .

3 *My favourite hobby is* _____ .

4 *My favourite sport is* _____ .

[1] **cooking** *Kochen*

 tal quiz **Ich kann** Kinder in einer britischen Schule verstehen.

Time for school

---

1 Listening **At school**

a) Before you listen **Look at the photo. Point and say the names of the students.**
Sieh dir das Foto an. Zeige auf die Kinder und sage ihre Namen.

🔊
1.11

b) Listen and draw lines. *Höre zu und ziehe Verbindungslinien.*

1 Zane		a is scared of the school.
2 Lily		b likes the tie.
4 Noah		c are students in class 7C.
5 Noah and Sunita		d is tired.

---

2 Speaking **School uniform**

What do you think of the school uniform?
Wie findest du die Schuluniform?

Good to know

In britischen Schulen tragen Kinder eine Schuluniform, die oft aus einem Blazer und einem Schlips besteht.

*The uniform is cool.
I like it.*

*I don't like the uniform.
It's horrible.*

3 Words **School things**

🔊 1.12 **a)** **Listen and point at Sunita's school things.**
Höre zu und zeige auf Sunitas Schulsachen.

🔊 1.13 **b)** **Listen to the words and repeat.** *Höre die Wörter und wiederhole.*

4 Looking at language **a / an**

Look at the picture in 3a) again. Write a or an.
Schau dir das Bild in 3a) noch einmal an. Schreibe a oder an.

1 *a* rubber   3 *an* exercise book   5 *an* English book

2 *a* glue stick   4 *a* pencil case   6 *a* ruler

5 I can remember

Sieh dir die Sachen auf Sunitas Schreibtisch genau an. Mach das Buch zu.
An welche Gegenstände auf Sunitas Schreibtisch kannst du dich erinnern?

A pen.

A ruler.

▶ **Extra practice 1–2, pp. 38–39**

---

[1] **glue stick** *Klebestift*   [2] **orange** *Orange*   [3] **pencil sharpener** *Bleistiftanspitzer*

6 Speaking **Noah's desk**

What can you see on Noah's desk? *Was siehst du auf Noahs Schreibtisch?*

> *A pencil case.*

> *Two brown pencils.*

a desk
a pencil case
an English book
a pencil sharpener
a glue stick
a rubber
an exercise book
a ruler
a pen
a pencil

▶ Wordbank 1, p. 169 ▶ Wordbank 2, p. 169

7 Reading **Hello, class 7C!**

1.14

a) Read and find the students in the picture. Write the numbers.
Lies den Text und finde Emma, Ravi und Layla im Bild. Schreibe die Nummern auf.

Emma 1

Layla 3

Ravi 2

Mr Lee __ Hello, class 7C! I'm Mr Lee, your class teacher and English teacher.
Emma __ Sorry I'm late, Mr Lee.
Mr Lee __ Ok, please sit down.
Ravi ___ Can I open the window, please?
Mr Lee __ Yes, you can.
Layla ___ Can I go to the toilet?
Mr Lee __ Yes, you can.
Please take your pencil case and your exercise book. Let's start!

b) Act out the conversation. *Spielt das Gespräch nach.*

8 Speaking **In class**

a) **Listen and draw lines.** *Höre zu und ziehe Verbindungslinien.*

1.15

1 What page is it?		a Yes, I can.
2 I don't understand exercise 1.		b It's page 9.
3 Can you help me with question 2?		c The answer is b.
4 What's the answer to question 3?		d Let's ask Mr Lee.
5 Can I use your book?		e Yes, here you are.

b) **Listen to the sentences in a).**
   Say the answers. *Höre dir die*
   Sätze in a) an. Beantworte sie.

1.16

c) **Walk around** **Practise the sentences**
   in a) with different partners. *Übe die*
   Sätze in a) mit unterschiedlichen
   Partnerinnen und Partnern.

   ▶ **Extra practice 3, p. 39**

My task

9 My classroom questions and answers

a) **Write new sentences. Change the parts in blue in 8a). Practise with a partner.**
   Schreibe neue Sätze. Verändere die Teile in Blau in 8a). Arbeitet zu zweit.

What page is it?

It's page 12.

I don't understand
exercise 5.

English

Let's ask
Mrs Pohl.

b) **Present your dialogue to another pair.** *Stellt euren Dialog einem anderen Paar vor.*

My timetable

1 The English lessons

🔊 1.17

a) **Read the dialogue.** *Lies den Dialog.*

Mr Lee	7C, please look at your timetable. Can you see the English lessons? They're in room 2.
Lily	Mr Lee, look at Tim. I think he's tired.
Mr Lee	You're right, Lily. And look at Emma. She's tired too. But it's break soon. It's in five minutes.

b) **Draw lines. Look at the words in blue in a). They can help you.**
Ziehe Verbindungslinien. Sieh dir die blauen Wörter in a) an. Sie helfen dir.

1 The English lessons are in room 2.		a It's in five minutes.
2 Tim is tired.		b They're in room 2.
3 Emma is tired too.		c He's tired.
4 Break is in five minutes.		d She's tired too.

2 People and things in class

Write. Use the words in the box.
Schreibe. Nutze die Wörter im Kasten.

~~he~~ • she • it • they

1	2	3	4

1 *he* _____ 2 *it* _____ 3 *they* _____ 4 *she* _____

3 Looking at language *am / is / are*

Erklär-
film

~~'m~~ • 's • 're

Füge die Apostrophe (') und die richtigen Formen
aus dem Kasten ein. Sieh dir S. 46 an, wenn du Hilfe brauchst.

1 I'm___ late.   2 You're___ busy.   3 He's___ tired. 4 She's___ tired too.
5 It's___ yellow.   6 We're___ in room 2.   7 They're___ in class 7C.

▶ Extra practice 4, p. 40

4 Varndean students and teachers

Write the correct letter A–D. *Schreibe den richtigen Buchstaben A–D.*

1 I'm an English teacher. B

2 We're tired. C

3 She's 12. A

4 They're in class 7C. D

5 Messages

Read the messages from Noah and his mum. Circle the right sentences.
Lies die Nachrichten von Noah und seiner Mutter. Umkreise die richtigen Sätze.

Hi, Mum! I like the classroom. (1) *It's big.* / She's big.

I like Mr Lee, my teacher, too. (2) We're cool. / *He's cool.*

And I like my new friends. (3) She's nice. / *They're nice.* ☺

Cool! Varndean School is big.

(4) They're a good school. / *It's a good school.*

Sorry, (5) *I'm busy.* / they're busy. Bye! ☺

▶ Extra practice 5–6, pp. 40–41

6 Song **Days of the week**

1.18

a) Words **Look at the days. Listen to the song. Put the days in the right order.**
Sieh dir die Wochentage an. Höre dir das Lied an. Setze die Wochentage in die richtige Reihenfolge.

Monday 1   Tuesday 2   Wednesday 3

Sunday 7   Thursday 4   Friday 5   Saturday 6

b) **Sing the song.** *Singe das Lied.*

7 Words **School subjects**

a) **Write the missing numbers.** *Schreibe die fehlenden Nummern.*

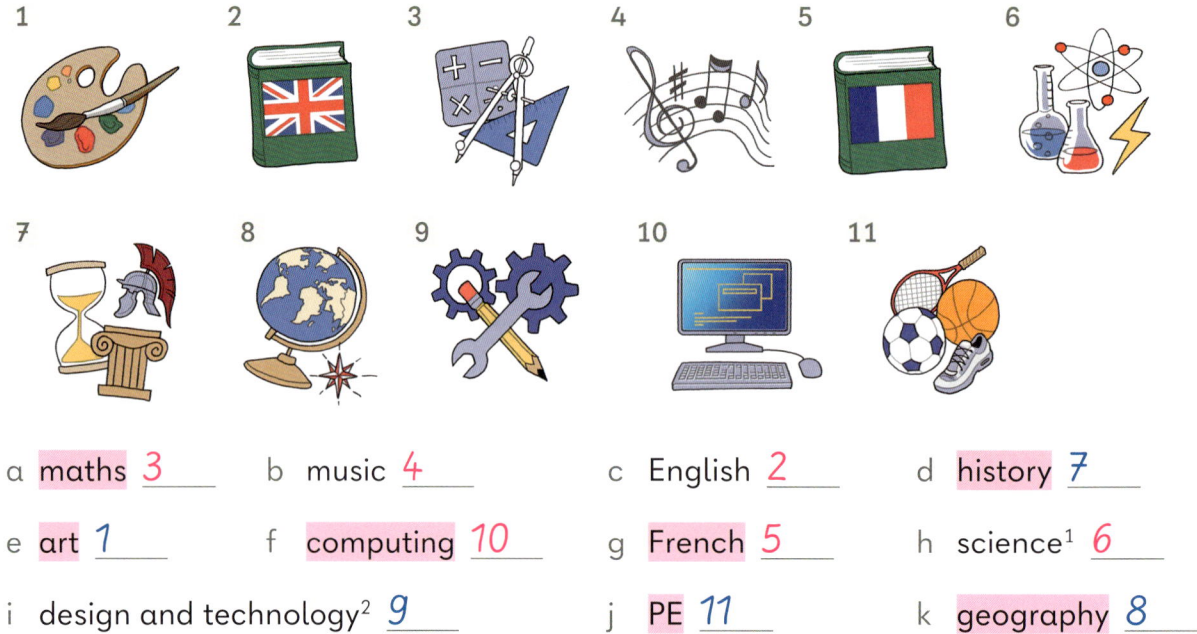

a maths *3*   b music *4*   c English *2*   d history *7*

e art *1*   f computing *10*   g French *5*   h science[1] *6*

i design and technology[2] *9*   j PE *11*   k geography *8*

🔊 1.19 b) **Listen and check.** *Höre zu und überprüfe.*

8 Listening **7C's timetable**

🔊 1.20 **Listen to Lily and Zane. Draw lines.** *Höre Lily und Zane zu. Verbinde.*

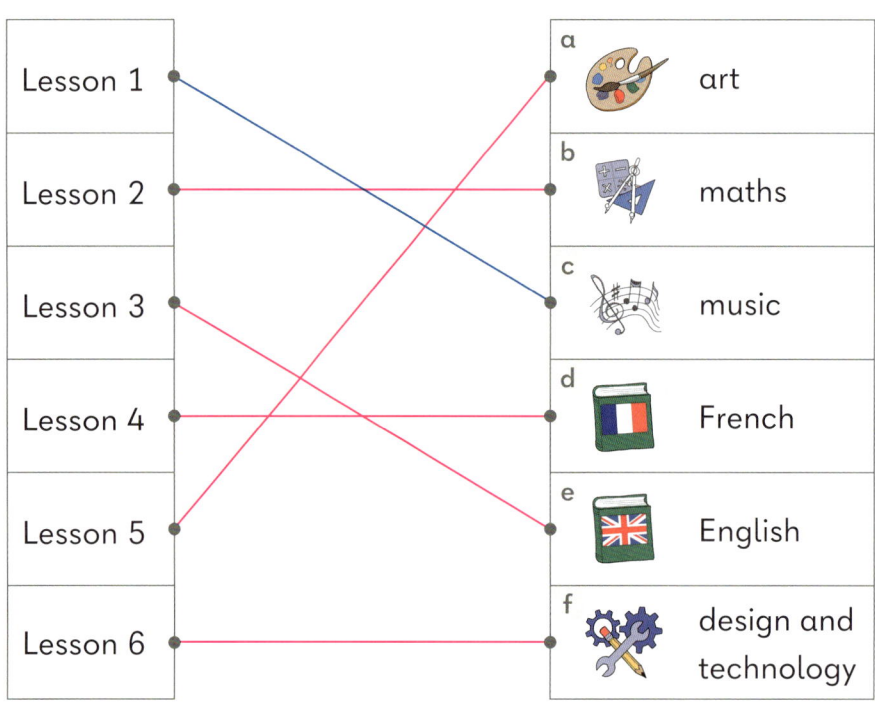

▶ Extra practice 7, p. 41

---

[1] **science** *Naturwissenschaft*   [2] **design and technology** *Werken, Werkunterricht*

9 The timetable song

1.22

a) Listen. Stand up when you hear a school subject.

Höre zu. Stehe auf, wenn du ein Schulfach hörst.

b) Listen again. In what order do you hear the subjects? Write 1–5.

Höre noch einmal zu. In welcher Reihenfolge hörst du die Fächer? Schreibe 1–5.

5___ 3___ 1___ 4___ 2___

10 Speaking **Favourite subjects**

▶ Wordbank 5, p. 172

a) Write about your favourite subjects. *Schreibe über deine Lieblingsschulfächer.*

I like *(computing)*_____. I don't like *(history)*_____.

My favourite subject is *(French)*_____.

b) Speed dating Make two lines. Talk to a partner.

Macht zwei Reihen. Sprecht mit eurem Gegenüber.

My task

11 My timetable

Write your timetable in English in your exercise book.

Schreibe deinen Stundenplan auf Englisch in dein Heft.

	Monday	Tuesday	Wednesday	Thursday	Friday
1					
2					
3					

▶ Wordbank 5, p. 172

It's a big school!

1 Words **Places at school**

🔊 1.23

a) **Look at the pictures. Read the conversation and complete the words.**
Sieh dir die Bilder an. Lies das Gespräch und vervollständige die Wörter.

c _a_ nt _e_ _e_ n   c _o_ mp _u_ t _e_ r room   sp _o_ rts hall   _a_ rt room

Noah ____ I'm hungry. Where's the canteen?
Sunita ____ This room isn't the canteen, it's the **art room**.
Noah ____ This is the **computer room**. And the toilets are here.
Lily ____ Look at this map! We're in building 1.
The canteen and the **sports** hall are in building 2. It's a big school!
Noah ____ They aren't in this building. We aren't near the canteen!
Sunita ____ I'm not hungry and I have two sandwiches. You can have one.
Noah ____ You aren't hungry, Sunita … I'm always hungry! Thanks!

🔊 1.24

b) **Listen and repeat the places.** *Höre zu und wiederhole die Räume.*

2 **What's right?**

Read 1a) again. Tick (✓) the right sentences.
Lies 1a) noch einmal. Mache ein Häkchen (✓) neben die richtigen Sätze.

1 Noah: I'm hungry. ☑
I'm not hungry. ☐

2 Lily: We're in building 1. ☑
We aren't in building 1. ☐

3 Noah: We're near the canteen. ☐
We aren't near the canteen. ☑

4 Noah: You're hungry, Sunita. ☐
You aren't hungry, Sunita. ☑

Erklär-film

3 Looking at language *am / is / are (negative)*

Draw lines. *Ziehe Verbindungslinien.*

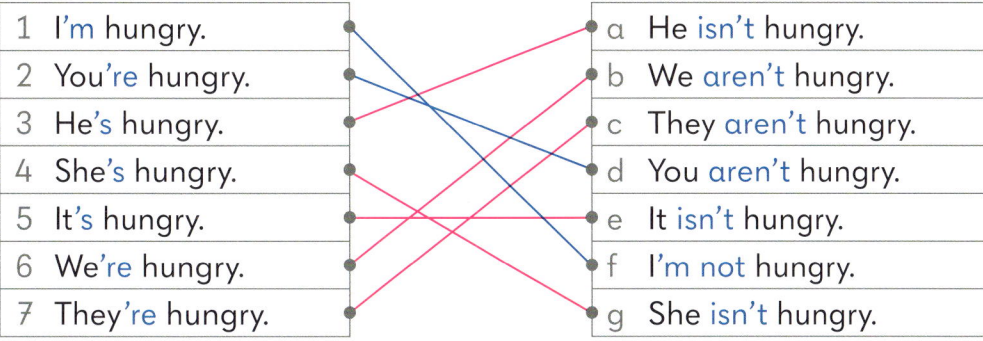

1 I'm hungry.	a He isn't hungry.
2 You're hungry.	b We aren't hungry.
3 He's hungry.	c They aren't hungry.
4 She's hungry.	d You aren't hungry.
5 It's hungry.	e It isn't hungry.
6 We're hungry.	f I'm not hungry.
7 They're hungry.	g She isn't hungry.

4 The new school

(Circle) the right picture (a or b) for the sentence.
Umkreise das richtige Bild (a oder b) für den Satz.

1 The school isn't small.   2 We aren't scared!

3 I'm happy at my school.   4 My new school is cool!

▶ Extra practice 8, p. 42

My task

5 My school

Read Lily's text. Change the words in blue and write sentences about you and your school. *Lies Lilys Text. Ändere die Wörter in Blau und schreibe Sätze über dich und deine Schule.*

My school is Varndean school.
I'm in class 7B.
My class teacher is Mr Lee.
My favourite place at school is the art room.
My favourite subject is English.
My school is cool.

▶ Digital help    ▶ Wordbank 6, p. 173

ital quiz **Ich kann** meine Schule beschreiben.

After school

1 Before you read **Look at the pictures. Who can you see?**
Sieh dir die Bilder an. Wen siehst du?

Zane, …

2 Reading **After school**

🔊 1.25

Read and listen to the story. *Lies die Geschichte und höre zu.*

Lily ____ Hey, Zane! Let's go to
the beach!
Zane ____ Sorry, I'm busy! Bye!
Lily ____ Zane is always busy.
Sunita __ You're right.

Kyle ____ You're too slow[1], Noah!
Jade ____ Noah is so weird.
Noah ____ I'm not weird!
Lily ____ Who are they?
Sunita __ They aren't from Varndean.
They're bullies[2].

Lily ____ That's Noah from our class.
He's in trouble[3]!
Sunita __ Can we help him?
Lily ____ I don't know.
I'm scared of bullies.

Noah ____ Hello, seagull. You're nice.
But the bullies aren't nice.
They're mean!
I'm sad. They think I'm weird.
But I'm not weird.
I'm Noah and I'm clever!

---

[1] **slow** *langsam*   [2] **bullies** *Mobber, Mobberinnen*   [3] **in trouble** *in Schwierigkeiten*

1.26

5

Lily ____ Oh no! Noah is sad.

Sunita __ Let's help him!

6

Jade ____ Look! The weird boy is still[1] here!

Sunita __ Stop! He's our friend.

Lily ____ Go away![2]

7

Here are my friends!

Noah ___ That's my friend, the seagull!
And her friends[3] too – they're
very helpful[4].

Kyle ____ Ugh! Let's go!

Jade ____ The seagulls are horrible!

8

Noah ___ Thanks. You're good friends.

Sunita __ That seagull is very clever!
You're good with animals,
Noah.

9

Noah __ Hi, Dad. These are my friends.

Dad ____ Hello! Nice to meet you.
This is Noah's dog, Buddy.
He's very friendly[5].

Lily ____ He's cool!

---

[1] **still** *(immer) noch*   [2] **Go away!** *Geht weg! Haut ab!*   [3] **her friends** *ihre Freunde*
[4] **helpful** *hilfsbereit*   [5] **friendly** *freundlich*

3 Words **Adjectives**

a) Match the English and German words. Draw lines.

Ziehe Linien zwischen den englischen und den passenden deutschen Wörtern.

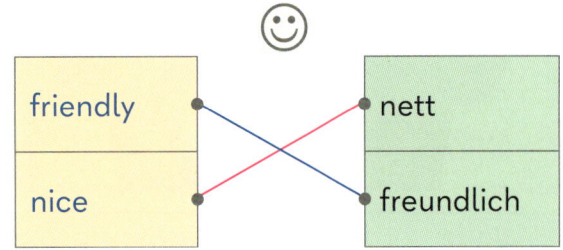

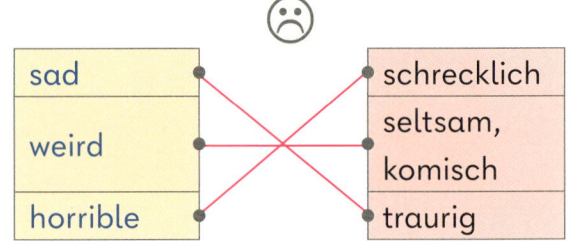

b) Write the correct word from a). *Schreibe das richtige Wort aus a).*

1 Kyle and Jade are _horrible_ to Noah.

2 Noah is _sad_.

3 Sunita and Lily are _nice_ to Noah.

4 Noah isn't _weird_.

5 Noah's dog is _friendly_.

4 Showtime **Action!**

Lest die Geschichte auf den Seiten 30–31 *mit verteilten Rollen. Spielt sie vor.*

5 Speaking **What's your opinion?**

Talk about the people in the story. Use the words in 3a).

Unterhaltet euch über die Personen in der Geschichte. Nutzt die Wörter aus 3a).

I like Sunita. She's nice.

I don't like Jade. She's horrible.

6 Life skills **Your best friend**

a) Read Noah's sentences about his best friend.

Lies Noahs Beschreibung über seinen besten Freund.

My best friend is my dog Buddy.

He's clever. He isn't horrible.

b) Write sentences about your best friend.

Schreibe Sätze über deinen besten Freund oder deine beste Freundin.

Digital quiz    **Ich kann** eine Geschichte über eine Freundschaft verstehen. ✓

The Brighton dares: At school

1 The two dares

Before you watch **Daisy and Emir do funny dares.**
Match the dares to the pictures. Write A–C.
Daisy und Emir machen lustige Mutproben.
Ordne die Mutproben den Bildern zu. Schreibe A–C.

1 Wear a beard[1] _C_

2 Speak backwards[2] _A_

3 Walk backwards _B_

A "old years eleven am I"

B

C

2 Viewing **At school**

a) *Sieh dir das Video von 00:00 bis 02:17 an. Welche Mutprobe hat Daisy für Emir?*
Welche Mutproben hat Emir für Daisy? Sieh dir die Bilder A–C aus 1 an. Schreibe A,
B und C.

Daisy's dare[3] for Emir: _C_   Emir's dares for Daisy: _A_ and _B_ .

b) **Watch all the video. (Circle) the right words.**
Sieh dir das gesamte Video an. Umkreise die richtigen Wörter.

1 It's Monday / (Friday).

2 The headteacher[4] is (Mr Campbell) / Mrs Collins .

3 Emily is in Room 12 / (the school garden).

3 My opinion

What do you think about the dares? Use words from the box.
Was denkst du über die Mutproben? Nutze die Wörter aus der Box.

cool • clever • funny[5] • good • mean • weird

1 I think the beard dare is *(funny)* .

2 I think the backwards dare is *(cool)* .

---

[1] **wear a beard** *einen Bart tragen*   [2] **backwards** *rückwärts*   [3] **dare** *Mutprobe*
[4] **headteacher** *Schulleiter/in*   [5] **funny** *lustig*

Learning vocabulary

1 Writing topic lists

Schreibe mehr Wörter in die Listen.

in my school bag (in meiner Schultasche)	school subjects (Fächer)	places at school (Räume in meiner Schule)
pen	maths	canteen
(pencil)	(English)	(classroom)
(ruler)	(PE)	(toilets)
(pencil case)	(history)	(art room)
(book)	(art)	(computer room)
(rubber)		

▶ Extra practice 9, p. 42

2 Test your partner

Arbeitet zu zweit. Schaut euch die Vokabeln auf den Seiten 43–47 an. Verdeckt die englischen Wörter und lest die deutschen Wörter vor. Kennt ihr die englischen Wörter noch?

3 Game **New words**

a) *Schreibe Wörter aus deinem Vocabulary auf Karteikarten.*

b) *Schreibe das englische Wort auf eine Seite der Karteikarte und die deutsche Bedeutung auf die Rückseite.*

c) *Wenn du möchtest, kannst du die Karteikarten schön gestalten, ein Bild dazu zeichnen oder ein Foto aufkleben.*

d) *Spielt in Gruppen. Alle legen ihre Kärtchen auf den Tisch und ziehen eine Karte. Kennt ihr die Übersetzung? Überprüft mit der Übersetzung auf der Rückseite.*

Digital quiz **Ich kann** Vokabeln auf unterschiedliche Weise lernen.

Make a poster about your school

Step 1

Erstelle ein Poster über dich und deine Schule. Schreibe zuerst auf Englisch:

▶ Wordbank 5, p. 172 ▶ Wordbank 6, p. 173 ▶ Digital help 🔽

A Was hast du in deiner Schultasche?

In my school bag I have *a book,* *(a pencil case, a rubber, a pen)* .

B Nenne eine Lehrkraft und schreibe auf, welches Fach sie unterrichtet.

(Mr Kato) is my *(music)* teacher.

C Nenne zwei Räume in eurem Schulgebäude.

(sports hall) *(computer room)*

D Welches Fach magst du? Welches Fach magst du nicht?

☺ I like *(English)* . ☹ I don't like *(PE)* .

Step 2

Schreibe alles von A–D auf dein Poster. Zeichne Bilder oder klebe Fotos dazu.

1.27 **1** Listening **At break**

Listen. What's the right order? Write 2–4.

Höre zu. Was ist die richtige Reihenfolge? Schreibe 2–4.

toilet *4*   basketball *2*   canteen *3*   beach *1*

2 Speaking **Mr Lee's desk**

What can you see in the picture? *Was siehst du auf dem Bild?*

A white computer.

3 Words **In the classroom**

(Circle) **the right word.** *Umkreise das richtige Wort.*

1 Can you (help)/ say me?
2 Can I answer / (open) the window?
3 (Sorry) / Please I'm late.
4 I don't take / (understand) the question.

Check

4 Language **Sunita's email**

Choose the right word. *Wähle das richtige Wort.*

Hi, Jasmine!

How _are_ you? | are • ~~is~~

I'_m_ in class 7C. | 're • 'm

My timetable _is_ cool. | is • am

English lessons _are_ on Mondays and Fridays. | is • are

And PE _is_ on Thursdays. | are • is

_Is_ your timetable OK? | Am • Is

Bye, Sunita.

5 Language **Jasmine's school**

Sieh dir das Bild an. Was ist richtig?
Setze das richtige Wort ein.

aren't • isn't

1 The students _aren't_ in the building.

2 The uniform tie _isn't_ black.

3 The classrooms _aren't_ near the canteen.

4 The sports hall _isn't_ in building 1.

6 Writing **My school**

Ergänze die Sätze über deine Schule.

The name of my school is _(Gesamtschule am Niederrhein)_ .

It's in _(Krefeld)_ .

My class teacher is _(Mrs Pohl)_ .

My favourite subject is _(music)_ .

Check

▶ page 21

Extra practice 1

Was siehst du in Lilys Rucksack? Mache ein Häkchen (✓) bei den richtigen Sachen und ein Kreuz (✗) bei den falschen Sachen. Schreibe die richtigen Sachen daneben.

a history book	✓	
a French book	✗	*an English book*
a maths book	✓	
a black ruler	✗	*a brown ruler*
an orange pencil case	✓	
a green exercise book	✗	*a pink exercise book*
three sandwiches	✗	*two sandwiches*

Extra practice 2   ▶ page 21

Look at Yasin's desk. What can you see? *Sieh dir Yasins Tisch an. Was siehst du?*

An English book, (three exercise books, pencils, a pen, a rubber, a pencil case, a rubber, an apple)

_____ .

Extra practice 3   ▶ page 23

Put the words in the right order. *Setze die Wörter in die richtige Reihenfolge.*

1 page • is • What • it

What page is it ?

2 don't • I • understand

I don't understand .

3 me • you • Can • help

Can you help me ?

4 I • use • Can • book • your

Can I use your book ?

Extra practice 4

▶ page 24

Complete the sentences with the words in the box.

Ergänze die Sätze mit den Wörtern im Kasten.

I • You • ~~He~~ • She • It • We • They

1 **Zane** is from Brighton. He ’s cool.

2 **Noah and Sunita** are good students. They ’re clever.

3 **Lily** is nice. She ’s in class 7C.

4 **Noah and I** are in class 7C. We ’re friends.

5 You ’re right, Lily.

6 **Break** is soon. It ’s in five minutes.

7 I ’m tired.

Extra practice 5

▶ page 25

Write names of students in your class.

Schreibe die Namen deiner Mitschülerinnen und Mitschüler auf.

1 She’s in a football team. ______

2 He’s clever. ______

3 He can draw. ______

4 She’s 11 years old. ______

5 She’s nice. ______

6 They’re good friends. ______ and ______

7 They like snakes. ______ and ______

▶ page 25

Extra practice 6

Complete Zane's message to a friend in London. Use 'm, 's, 're.

Ergänze Zanes Nachricht an eine Freundin in London. Nutze 'm, 's, 're.

Hi, Zara!

How are you?

I '*m* fine.

It '*s* nice in Brighton.

My new friend is Noah. He '*s* cool.

Noah and Sunita are in class 7C.

I '*m* in 7B.

I like Sunita. She '*s* nice.

▶ page 26

Extra practice 7

🔊 1.21

What are their favourite subjects? Listen. Circle the right subject.

Was sind ihre Lieblingsfächer? Höre zu. Umkreise das richtige Schulfach.

1 Sunita A  science B  English

2 Lily A  music B  art

3 Noah A  maths B  French

4 Zane A  PE B  history

▶ page 29

Extra practice 8

Look at the pictures. Put the words in the right order to make sentences.
Sieh dir die Bilder an. Setze die Wörter in die richtige Reihenfolge.

1

1 big. • The dog • is

The dog is big.

2

2 nice. • are • Lily and Noah

Lily and Noah are nice.

3

3 isn't • The book • new.

The book isn't new.

4

4 are • The sandwiches • good.

The sandwiches are good.

▶ page 34

Extra practice 9

Underline the words in the right colour.
Unterstreiche die Wörter in der richtigen Farbe.

uniform	subjects	school things	days	places at school
pen grün	English gelb	tie blau	Friday rot	exercise book grün
geography gelb	rubber grün	toilet schwarz	computer grün	classroom schwarz
pencil case grün	Thursday rot	blazer blau	music gelb	

🔊 **Hello!**

Hello! I'm Scout, the seagull.

▶ p. 10	I	ich
	I'm (= I am)	ich bin
	a seagull	eine Möwe
	hungry	hungrig
	Scout is	Scout ist
	from Hove	aus Hove
	year	das Jahr; der Jahrgang
	old	alt
	Scout is six years old.	Scout ist sechs (Jahre alt).
	six	sechs —————————→
▶ p. 11	Hello.	Hallo. / Servus.
	the	der, die, das
	What's your name?	Wie heißt du?
	your	dein/e; euer/eure; Ihr/e
	How old are you?	Wie alt bist du?
	you	du; dich; dir; ihr; euch; Sie; Ihnen
	Where are you from?	Wo kommst du her?
	What about you?	Und du? / Was ist mit dir?
	Hi.	Hallo.
	(to) like	mögen
	football	der Fußball
	you're (= you are)	du bist; ihr seid; Sie sind
	thank you, thanks	danke (schön)
▶ p. 12	mum	die Mama, die Mutti
	Leo's mum	die Mama / die Mutti von Leo
	ball	Ball
	boy	der Junge
	girl	das Mädchen
	thing	das Ding, die Sache
	(to) eat	essen; fressen
	things to eat	Dinge zum Essen
	animal	das Tier
	here's	hier ist
	can	können
	(to) see	sehen
	dog	der Hund
	(to) remember	sich erinnern an
	and	und

1 one	**2** two	**3** three
4 four	**5** five	**6** six
7 seven	**8** eight	**9** nine
10 ten	**11** eleven	**12** twelve
13 thirteen	**14** fourteen	

▶ p. 14	horse	das Pferd
	an elephant	ein Elefant
	cat	die Katze
	lion	der Löwe
	monkey	der Affe
	parrot	der Papagei
	snake	die Schlange
	it's (= it is)	es ist *(bei Sachen und Tieren auch: er ist; sie ist)*
	my	mein/e
	favourite animal	das Lieblingstier
	fish, *pl* fish	der Fisch
▶ p. 15	drawing	das Zeichnen
	listening to music	Musik (an)hören
	swimming	das Schwimmen
	taking photos	das Fotografieren *(Hobby)*
	sport	der Sport; die Sportart
	(to) love	lieben, sehr mögen
	hobby	das Hobby
	I don't like football.	Ich mag Fußball nicht. / Ich mag keinen Fußball.
	small	klein
	black	schwarz
	big	groß
	gold	das Gold; goldfarben
	silver	das Silber; silberfarben
▶ p. 16	colour	die Farbe
	hat	der Hut, die Mütze
▶ p. 17	(to) stand up	aufstehen
	(to) sit down	sich hinsetzen
	(to) open	öffnen; aufschlagen *(Buch)*
	book	das Buch
	(to) put your hand up	sich melden, aufzeigen
	hand	die Hand
	everybody	jeder; alle
	Hello everybody!	Hallo/Servus allerseits!

a – an

a dog   **an e**lephant
a good picture   **an o**ld picture

! one **fish** – two **fish**

colours

black schwarz   **blue** blau   **brown** braun
purple violett, lila   **orange** orange
green grün   **grey** grau   **pink** pink, rosa
red rot   **yellow** gelb   **white** weiß

hats

Unit 1 – My new school

Topic 1

▶ p. 20	(to) **be scared (of)**	Angst haben (vor)
	of	von
	school	die Schule
	tie	die Krawatte
	student	der Schüler, die Schülerin
	class	die Klasse
	tired	müde
	(school) uniform	die (Schul-)Uniform
	horrible	schrecklich
▶ p. 21	**exercise book**	das Schulheft, das Übungsheft
	English	Englisch; englisch
	pencil	der Bleistift
	apple	der Apfel
	pencil case	das Federmäppchen
	pen	der Kugelschreiber, der Stift; der Füller
	rubber	das Radiergummi
	ruler	das Lineal
	desk	der Schreibtisch
▶ p. 22	**Mr** Lee	Herr Lee
	teacher	der Lehrer, die Lehrerin
	Sorry. / I'm sorry.	Tut mir leid. / Entschuldigung.
	I'm late.	Ich habe mich verspätet.
	window	das Fenster
	yes	ja
	(to) **go**	gehen; fahren
	toilet	die Toilette
	Let's …, Let us …	Lass uns …/ Lasst uns …
	(to) **start**	beginnen, anfangen (mit)
▶ p. 23	**page (p.)**	die (Buch-/Heft-)Seite
	(to) **understand**	verstehen
	exercise	die Übung, die Aufgabe
	(to) help	helfen
	me	mir; mich
	with	mit; bei

Are you **tired**?

school uniforms

yes ◄► no (nein)

question	die Frage
(to) **use**	benutzen, verwenden
answer	die Antwort
(to) **ask**	fragen
Here you are.	Bitte schön. / Hier, bitte. ⟶
Mrs Pohl	Frau Pohl

Yes, here you are.

Can I use your book, please?

Topic 2

▶ p. 24	(to) **look at** sb./sth.	jn. anschauen; sich etwas anschauen
	at	an; in; bei; auf
	timetable	der Stundenplan
	lesson	die (Unterrichts-)Stunde
	they're (= they are)	sie sind
	they aren't	sie sind nicht

I'm (I am) – ich bin	**I'm not** – ich bin nicht
you're (you are) – du bist; ihr seid	**you aren't** – du bist nicht, ihr seid nicht
he's (he is) – er ist	**he isn't** – er ist nicht
she's (she is) – sie ist	**she isn't** – sie ist nicht
we're (we are) – wir sind	**we aren't** – wir sind nicht
they're (they are) – sie sind	**they aren't** – sie sind nicht

room	der Raum, das Zimmer
(to) **think**	denken, meinen, glauben
(to) **be right**	Recht haben
too	auch
but	aber
break	die Pause
soon	bald
minute	die Minute
(to) **be busy**	beschäftigt sein, (viel) zu tun haben

▶ p. 25	**classroom**	das Klassenzimmer
	new	neu
	friend	der Freund, die Freundin	**friendly** = freundlich
	nice	nett, schön

Monday (der) Montag	**Tuesday** (der) Dienstag	**Wednesday** (der) Mittwoch
Thursday (der) Donnerstag	**Friday** (der) Freitag	**Saturday** (der) Samstag
Sunday (der) Sonntag	❗ Die Wochentage werden immer großgeschrieben.	

▶ p. 26	**maths**	die Mathe(matik)
	history	die Geschichte (*vergangene Zeiten*)
	French	Französisch; französisch
	PE	der (Schul-)Sport
	art	die Kunst

geography	die Geografie, die Erdkunde
computing	die Informatik
▶ p. 27 subject	das (Schul-)Fach

Topic 3

▶ p. 28 canteen	die Kantine, die (Schul-)Mensa
this	dies; diese(r, s)
map	die Landkarte, der (Stadt-)Plan
hall	die Halle, der Saal
building	das Gebäude
near	nahe (bei), in der Nähe von
(to) have	haben
always	immer
▶ p. 29 happy	glücklich, froh
place	der Ort, der Platz

Story

▶ p. 30 beach	der Strand
so weird	so seltsam, so komisch
who?	wer?
that	das (dort)
our	unser/e
him	ihm, ihn
her	sie, ihr
(to) know	wissen; kennen
mean	gemein, fies
sad	traurig
▶ p. 31 no	nein
very big	sehr groß
dad	der Papa, der Vati
These are my friends.	Das hier sind meine Freunde/Freundinnen.
Nice to meet you.	Freut mich, dich/euch/Sie kennenzulernen.
▶ p. 32 best	beste(r, s); am besten

Unit 2
My family and home

Meera

Ben   Willow

Nish

Priya Rahi Anika Jay grandpa grandma

◀)) 1.28

1 Words **Sunita's family**

a) **Look at the photos. Listen to Sunita and Lily. Point at the people.**
Schau dir die Fotos an. Höre Sunita und Lily zu. Zeige auf die Menschen.

b) **Match. Then listen again and check your answers.**
Ordne zu. Dann höre noch einmal zu und überprüfe deine Antworten.

1 Nish is my		A uncle.
2 Meera is my		B partner.
3 Ben is Meera's		C brother.
4 Rahi is my		D aunt.
5 Priya is my		E mum.

Nach dieser Unit kann ich ...

- ○ über meine Familie und unsere Haustiere sprechen
- ○ mein Zuhause und mein Zimmer beschreiben
- ○ Wörter buchstabieren

Unit task

- ○ mein Traumzimmer präsentieren

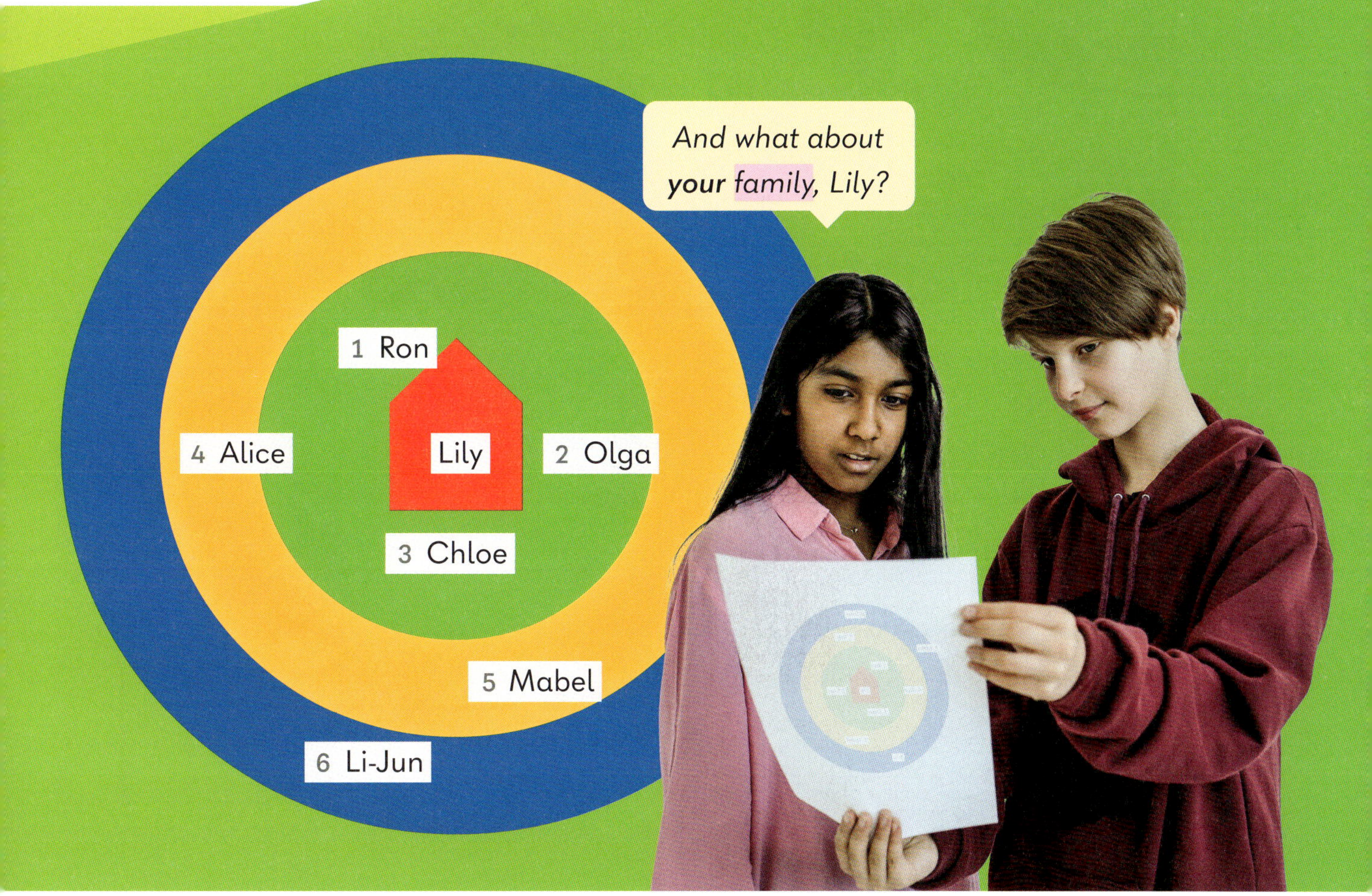

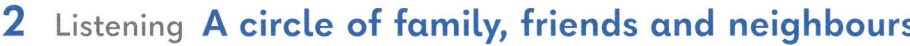

1 Ron
4 Alice
Lily
2 Olga
3 Chloe
5 Mabel
6 Li-Jun
And what about your family, Lily?

2 Listening **A circle of family, friends and neighbours**

1.29

a) **Look at Lily's circle and listen. Are these sentences right (✓) or wrong (✗)?**
Schau dir Lilys Kreis an und höre zu. Sind diese Sätze richtig (✓) oder falsch (✗)?

1 Ron is Lily's dad.	✓	2 Chloe is Lily's sister.	✓
3 Alice is Lily's cousin.	✗	4 Mabel is Lily's grandma.	✓

b) **Draw your circle of important people and tell a partner about them.** *Male deinen Kreis mit wichtigen Menschen und erzähle einer Partnerin oder einem Partner von ihnen.*

Anna is my mum. *Micha is my neighbour.*

► Extra practice 1, p. 72 ► Wordbank 7, p. 174

tal quiz **Ich kann über meine Familie sprechen.** ✓

My pets

a cat • (a fish) • a horse • a parrot •
a rabbit[1] • a snake • two hamsters[2]

1   Reading   **A lot of animals!**

a)   **Before you read**   *Eins von den Tieren im Kasten ist nicht im Bild. Finde dieses Tier.*

🔊 1.30

Scout ___	Hello, I'm Scout.
George _	Hi, I'm George.
Scout ___	Are you OK?
George _	No, I'm not. It's not quiet at home.
Scout ___	Are you angry?
George _	Yes, I am.
Scout ___	Is Sunita in your family?
George _	Yes, she is. Sunita's mum is a vet. It's the weekend and we have a lot of animals from Meera's work in our house.
Scout ___	Is that good?
George _	No, it isn't.
Scout ___	Oh. Are they too loud?
George _	Yes, they are. And the house is so messy!

b)   **Now tick (✓) the right sentence.** *Hake (✓) nun den richtigen Satz ab.*

1   a) George is happy.   ☐   b) George isn't happy.   ☑

2   a) The animals are loud.   ☑   b) The animals are tired.   ☐

3   a) George is Lily's pet.   ☐   b) George is in Sunita's house.   ☑

🔊 1.31

2   Words   **A cat, a fish ...**

Listen and repeat the words in 1a). *Höre zu und wiederhole die Wörter in 1a).*

---

[1] **rabbit** *Kaninchen*   [2] **hamster** *Hamster*

Erklär-
film

3 Looking at language **Questions and short answers**

a) **Look at the dialogue on page 50 again. Find the questions and complete them.** *Schau dir den Dialog auf Seite 50 noch einmal an. Finde die Fragen und ergänze sie.*

1 *Are* you OK?   4 *Is* that good?

2 *Are* you angry?   5 *Are* they too loud?

3 *Is* Sunita in your family?

b) **Match the questions and answers.** *Ordne die Fragen und Antworten einander zu.*

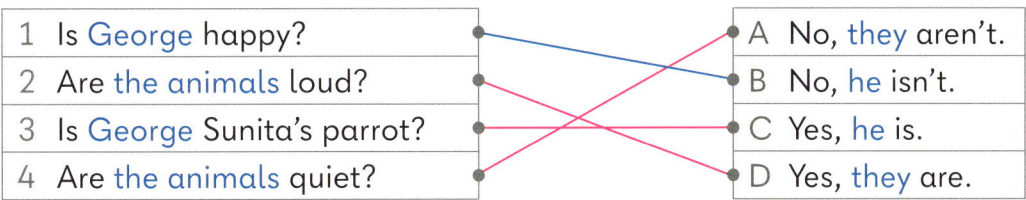

1 Is George happy?	A No, they aren't.
2 Are the animals loud?	B No, he isn't.
3 Is George Sunita's parrot?	C Yes, he is.
4 Are the animals quiet?	D Yes, they are.

4 Scout's questions

a) **Read the questions. (Circle) the answer that is true for you.**
Lies die Fragen. Umkreise die Antwort, die auf dich zutrifft.

1 Are you good with animals?   – Yes, I am. / No, I'm not.
2 Is your favourite animal friendly?   – Yes, it is. / No, it isn't.
3 Is it loud in your house?   – Yes, it is. / No, it isn't.
4 Are you scared of snakes?   – Yes, I am. / No, I'm not.
5 Are you and your family cat fans? – Yes, we are. / No, we aren't.

b) **Ask your partner the questions in a). Your partner answers. Then swap roles.**
Stelle deiner Partnerin oder deinem Partner die Fragen in a). Deine Partnerin oder dein Partner antwortet. Dann tauscht die Rollen.

Are you good with animals?

No, I'm not. What about you?

▶ Extra practice 2, p. 72

5 Listening **Is that your pet?**

a) Before you listen **What animals can you see in pictures 1 and 2?**
Welche Tiere kannst du auf den Bildern 1 und 2 sehen?

I can see …

b) **Listen. Write the picture number next to the correct name.**
Höre zu. Schreibe die Bildnummer neben den richtigen Namen.

1.32

Noah's pet *2*   Zane's pet *3*   Lily's pet *1*

c) **Listen again. Tick (✓) the answer you hear.**
Höre noch einmal zu. Hake (✓) die Antworten ab, die du hörst.

1.32

1 Are you OK, Sunita?	Yes, I am.	☐	No, I'm not.	✓
2 Is your dog Buddy loud?	Yes, he is.	☐	No, he isn't.	✓
3 Are you too busy for pets?	Yes, I am.	✓	No, I'm not.	☐
4 Are they your pets?	Yes, they are.	☐	No, they aren't.	✓

6 Words **A missing pet**

Complete the poster with the words from the box.
Ergänze das Poster mit Wörtern aus dem Kasten.

friendly • Please • ten • ~~orange~~

Our parrot is missing[1].

He's blue and *orange*   .

He's *ten*   years old.

He's very nice and *friendly*   .

Please   call[2] 07700 900426

if[3] you see him.

MISSING

! Im Englischen wird die Null oft als „oh" ausgesprochen.

---

[1] **missing** *vermisst*   [2] **call** *anrufen*   [3] **if** *wenn, falls*

7 Reading *FindAPet*

a) Before you read **Look at the photos. Which pet is your favourite?**
Schau dir die Fotos an. Welches ist dein Lieblingshaustier?

| Rex is a big and happy dog. He's very friendly, but he's very loud! He isn't mean. | Axel is a small, green lizard[1]. He's quiet and very friendly. He isn't slow. | Maude is old, but she is fast. She's cute. But she isn't friendly! |

b) **Read about Lily's dream pet. Which pet is right for her?**
Lies Lilys Text über ihr Traumhaustier.
Welches Haustier wäre für sie richtig?

Axel _____

> My dream pet[2] is fast.
> It's not big and it's not loud.

c) **Match the German words with the English words.**
Ordne die deutschen Wörter den englischen zu.

1	happy		freundlich
2	friendly		laut
3	loud		gemein
4	mean		glücklich

5	quiet		leise
6	slow		schnell
7	fast		langsam
8	cute		niedlich

My task

8 My dream pet

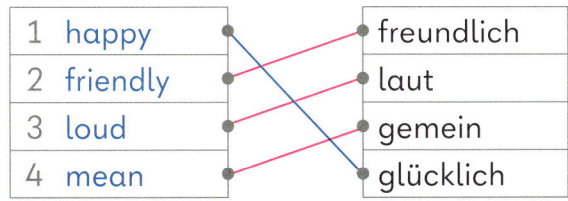

a) **Write about your dream pet.**
Use some of the words in 7c).

> My dream pet is a ...
> It's ... and ...

Schreibe über dein Traumhaustier. Verwende einige der Wörter in 7c).

▶ **Digital help** ▶ Wordbank 8, p. 175

b) **Tell a partner about your dream pet.**
Erzähle einer Partnerin / einem Partner von deinem Traumhaustier. ▶ **Extra Practice 3, p. 73**

¹ **lizard** *Eidechse* ² **dream pet** *Traumhaustier*

 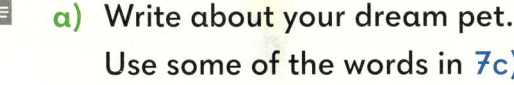

Different homes

1 Listening Four homes

a) Before you listen **Look at the photos. What can you see?** *Schau dir die Fotos an. Was siehst du?*

> *I can see a house and a garden.*

tree

garden

🔊 1.33 b) **Listen to Zane, Sunita, Lily and Noah. Where do they live? Write the number of the correct picture.** *Höre Zane, Sunita, Noah und Lily zu. Wo wohnen sie? Schreibe die Nummer des richtigen Bildes auf.*

flat

balcony

garage

Zane: *2*　　Sunita: *1*　　Lily: *3*　　Noah: *4*

🔊 1.33 2 About the homes

Listen again. Who says it? Zane (Z), Sunita (S), Noah (N) or Lily (L)?
Höre noch einmal zu. Wer sagt das? Zane (Z), Sunita (S), Noah (N) oder Lily (L)?

1 There's a balcony.　　L

2 There's a small garden.　　N

3 There are a lot of trees.　　S

4 There are two flats.　　Z

3 My home

Tick (✓) the sentences that are true for your home.
Hake (✓) die Sätze ab, die auf dein Zuhause zutreffen.

1 There's a balcony. ☐　　2 There's a garden. ☐　　3 It's a house. ☐

4 It's a flat. ☐　　5 It's big. ☐　　6 It's small. ☐

4 Viewing **A tour of Sunita's home**

a) **Before you watch** **What do you remember about Sunita's family and home?** *Sunitas Familie und Zuhause: woran erinnerst du dich?*

Sunita lives in …

Sunita's mum is a …

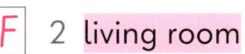

b) **Watch the tour of Sunita's home. Can you see Sunita's room?**
Schau dir den Rundgang durch Sunitas Haus an. Kannst du Sunitas Zimmer sehen?

5 Words **Rooms**

a) **Look at the picture of Sunita's house. What are the names of the rooms? Write A–G.** *Schau dir Sunitas Haus an. Wie heißen die Räume? Schreibe A–G.*

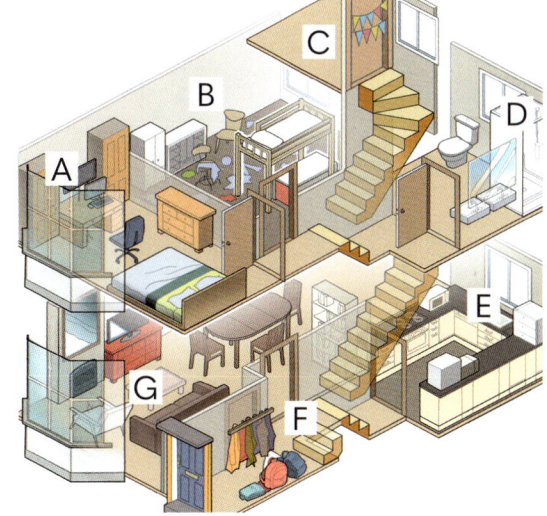

1 hall **F**   2 living room **G**

3 bathroom **D**   4 kitchen **E**

5 Meera's bedroom **A**   6 Nish's bedroom **B**

7 Sunita's bedroom **C**

b) **Watch the video again and check your answers.**
Schau dir das Video noch einmal an und überprüfe deine Antworten.

My task

6 My home

a) **Read Lily's text.** *Lies Lilys Text.*

> I live with my mum and dad. We live in a flat in Brighton. There's a kitchen, a bathroom, a living room. There are two bedrooms.

b) **Write about your home.**
Schreibe über dein Zuhause.

I live with my *(mum and my brother)* .

We live in a *(house)* in *(Stuttgart)* .

There's *(a kitchen)* , *(a bathroom)* and *(a living room)* .

There are *(three bedrooms)* .

▶ Digital help ↴   ▶ Wordbank 9, p. 175   ▶ Extra practice 4, p. 74

 tal quiz ↴   **Ich kann** mein Zuhause beschreiben. ✓

In my room

1   Speaking   **Sunita's room**

a)   **Look at the picture. What can you see?** *Schau dir das Bild an. Was siehst du?*

> *I can see …*   *There's a …*   *There are two / three …*

b)   **Right (✓) or wrong (✗)?** *Richtig (✓) oder falsch (✗)?*

1   There are two cushions on the bed. ✗   4   There's a green chair. ✓

2   There's a computer on the desk. ✓   5   There are two cushions on the sofa. ✓

3   There's a blue lamp. ✗   6   There's a robot on the sofa. ✗

---

2   Words   **Things in my room**

a)   **Find and ⟨circle⟩ at least five things from Sunita's room.**
Finde mindestens fünf Gegenstände aus Sunitas Zimmer und kreise sie ein.

R	O	B	O	T	X	L	A	M	P	Z
B	E	D	Z	C	U	S	H	I	O	N
C	O	M	P	U	T	E	R	X	Z	X
X	S	O	F	A	Z	C	H	A	I	R

🔊 **b)**   **Listen and repeat the words.** *Höre zu und wiederhole die Wörter.*   ▶ Extra practice 5, p. 75
1.34

3 Reading **Where is it?**

a) Before you read **Look at the picture of Sunita's room. Can you see Scout and George?** *Schau dir das Bild von Sunitas Zimmer an. Kannst du Scout und George sehen?*

b) **Read what Sunita says. Find the things in her room and (circle) them.**
Lies was Sunita sagt. Finde die Dinge in ihrem Zimmer und kreise sie ein.

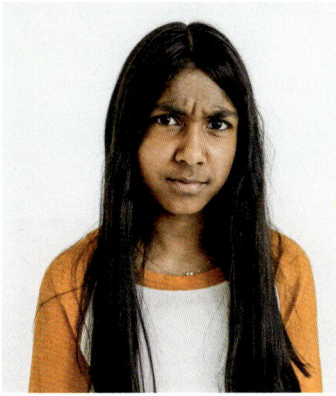

> Oh no! Look at my room! It's so messy!
> The cushions are on the floor[1].
> There's a book next to the lamp.
> And there's a book in front of the computer.
> I can see George behind the door.
> And I can see Scout under the bed!
> Robbie the robot is on the chair.
> Oh no! Where is my chocolate?

c) Opinion line **Is your room messy or tidy? Stand in a line. Then count the students.** *Ist dein Zimmer unordentlich oder aufgeräumt? Reihe dich an passender Stelle ein. Dann zählt die Schüler/innen.*

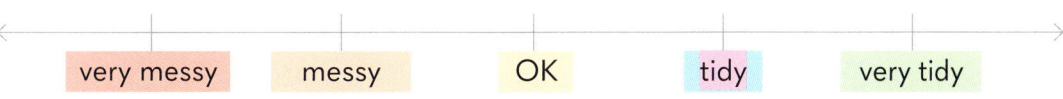

very messy   messy   OK   tidy   very tidy

d) **Talk about your results.**
Sprecht über eure Ergebnisse.

> Seven students have very messy rooms.   Five students ...

---

[1] **floor** *Fußboden*

4 Where's Scout?

Which picture goes with each sentence? Write A–F.
Welches Bild passt zu welchem Satz? Schreibe A–F.

1 Scout is next to the sandwich. **D**

2 Scout is on the cushion. **B**

3 Scout is in front of the computer. **F**

4 Scout is under the bed. **A**

5 Scout is behind the lamp. **E**

6 Scout is in the wardrobe. **C**

▶ Extra practice 6, p. 75

5 Question words

Match the questions and answers.
Ordne den Fragen die Antworten zu.

 who = *wer* • where = *wo* • what = *was*

| 1 Who is George? |
| 2 Where is George? |
| 3 What is George's favourite food[1]? |

| A It's apple. |
| B He's Sunita's pet. |
| C He's on the chair. |

6 Questions for you

Ask and answer the questions with a partner.
Stelle die Fragen und beantworte sie zusammen mit einer Partnerin/einem Partner.

Where is your home?	It's in …
Who is your favourite neighbour?	My favourite neighbour is …
What is your favourite room in your home?	My favourite room is …

[1] **food** *Futter*

7 Where are my things?

Read Sunita's questions. (Circle) the right question word.
Lies Sunitas Fragen. Kreise das richtige Fragewort ein.

1 (Where) / Who are my sandwiches?   – They're in the kitchen.

2 (Who) / Where has my blazer?   – Not me!

3 What / (Where) is my red tie?   – It's under the bed.

4 (What) / Who animals are in the house?   – A dog, a cat and a snake.

5 What / (Where) is the snake?   – It's in its terrarium.

▶ Extra practice 7–8, p. 76

My task

8 My room

There are three blue cushions on the bed.
There's a green lamp. There's a computer on the desk.

a) **Draw your room. Write words and sentences about your room.**
Male dein Zimmer. Schreibe Wörter und Sätze über dein Zimmer.

▶ Digital help
▶ Wordbank 9, p. 175

b) **Show your picture to your partner and talk about it.**
Zeige dein Bild deiner Partnerin oder deinem Partner
und sprich darüber.

---

 tal quiz    **Ich kann** mein Zimmer beschreiben.

At home with Sunita

🔊 **1**   Song **Ben's song**
1.35

Listen to Ben's song. Read sentences 1–3. ⟨Circle⟩ **the right word.**
Höre dir Bens Lied an. Lies die Sätze 1–3. Kreise das richtige Wort ein.

1 The flat is big /⟨small⟩.   2 It's ⟨old⟩/ new.   3 There are ⟨two⟩/ three bedrooms.

2   Reading **Sunita's problem**

a)   Before you read **How do the people in pictures 1–3 feel?**
Wie fühlen sich die Menschen auf den Bildern 1–3?

| angry • happy • |
| sad |

1 Sunita is *angry*____ .   2 Lily is *sad*____ .   3 Ben is *happy*____ .

🔊 b)   **Read Sunita and Lily's messages.** *Lies Sunitas und Lilys Nachrichten.*
1.36

> Hi, Lily. Are you at home? ✓

> Hi, Sunita. Yes, I am. I'm alone and it's very quiet 🙂. My parents are at work.   ✓

> It isn't quiet here! My mum is at work, but my brother is in his room. Willow is at her mum's house, but Ben is here. ✓

> Ben is nice, right? ✓

> Yes, he is. And he's a very good cook! But he's always in the living room with his guitar. And his music is horrible! ✓

> Talk to him! ✓

> But he's so nice. And mum is a big fan of his music. ✓

> Sorry, it's time for parkour now. Bye, Sunita. And remember: Talk to Ben! ✓

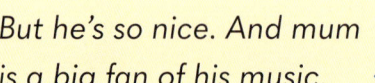

🔊 1.37

c) **Now it's time for dinner. Look at the pictures and listen. What is Sunita's problem? Tick (✓) the right answer.** *Jetzt ist es Zeit für das Abendessen. Schau die Bilder an und höre zu. Was ist Sunitas Problem? Hake (✓) die richtige Antwort ab.*

A Dinner is bad. ☐   B Nish is mean. ☐   C Ben's music is too loud. ☑

Let me play my new song!

It's horrible!

I can use headphones.

🔊 1.38

d) **Read the end of the story.** *Lies das Ende der Geschichte.*

Hi, Sunita. I'm home. ✓

Hi, Lily! Are you tired? ✓

Yes, I am! Is there still a problem with Ben's music? ✓

No, it's OK now. And not all Ben's music is bad. Listen to this 🎵 – it's for my video game. ✓

OK ... Wow! That's cool! ... Oh, mum is back at home now – time for dinner! 🙂 Bye! ✓

Bye, Lily. ✓

Home, sweet home!

3 Reading **The story**

Read the story again. Are these sentences right (✓) or wrong (✗)?
Lies die Story noch einmal. Sind diese Sätze richtig (✓) oder falsch (✗)?

1 Lily is alone at home.   ☑

2 Ben is a very good cook.   ☑

3 Sunita is a fan of Ben's music.   ☒

4 Nish is sorry.   ☑

5 Sunita thinks Ben's video game music is bad.   ☒

4 Who is it?

Ⓒircle the correct names.
Kreise die richtigen Namen ein.

1 Sunita / ⟨Lily⟩ is alone at home.   3 Nish / ⟨Ben⟩ is nice and a great cook.

2 ⟨Nish⟩ / Ben is in his room.   4 Ben / ⟨Sunita⟩ is angry about the loud music.

5 Words **New words**

Match the words and pictures.
Verbinde die Wörter und die dazu passenden Bilder.

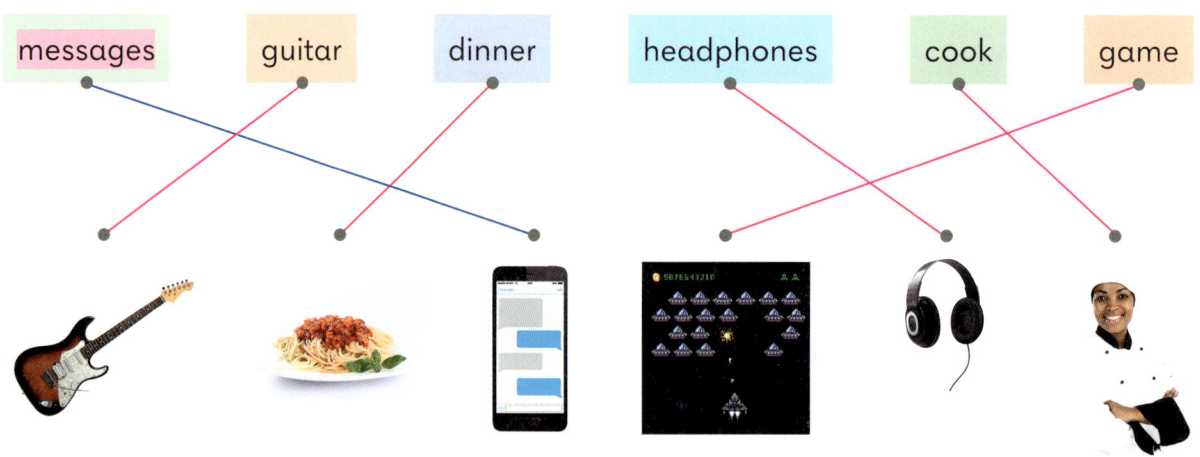

messages   guitar   dinner   headphones   cook   game

The Brighton dares: Family

1 What are the dares?

Before you watch **Look at the pictures and complete the sentences.**

Schau dir die Bilder an und ergänze die Sätze.

HUG

postbox

from · to

family tree

1 Dare[1] 1 is to h*ug* _____ a p*ostbox* _____ for t*wo* _____ hours[2].

2 Dare 2 is to make a 3D family *tree* _____ .

2 Viewing **Two families**

a) **Watch the video and put the pictures in the right order. Write 1–4.**

Schau dir das Video an und bringe die Fotos in die richtige Reihenfolge. Schreibe 1–4.

4

2

1

3

b) **Right (✓) or wrong (✗)?**

Richtig (✓) oder falsch (✗)?

1 Mr Campbell and Mrs Collins have letters[3] for the postbox. ✓

2 Mrs Collins wants to find her dad. ✗

3 Mrs Collins has tea[4] for Daisy after her dare. ✓

4 Emir does his dare on the beach. ✗

5 Mrs Collins and Robert Collins speak on the phone. ✓

---

[1] **dare** *Mutprobe* [2] **hour** *Stunde* [3] **letter** *Brief* [4] **tea** *Tee*

Spelling

1 Song **The alphabet**

1.39

a) **Listen and read.** *Höre zu und lies.*

b) **Sing or say the alphabet in pairs.**
Singt oder sagt das Alphabet zu zweit auf.
Partner A: die schwarzen Zeilen.
Partner B: die blauen Zeilen.

The alphabet song
A B C D E
F G H I J
K L M N O
P Q R S T
U V W
X Y Z
That's the alphabet!

2 Name, address and phone number

1.40

Listen and write the missing letters and numbers.
Höre zu und ergänze die fehlenden Buchstaben und Zahlen.

First name[1]:   SUNITA

Family name[2]:   C H A N D R A

Address[3]:   22 P A L M E I R A Road[4], Hove BN3 2JN

Phone number: 07700 9 0 0 5 6 7

3 Spell, write and say

a) *Suche zwei längere Wörter aus der Vokabelliste (Seiten 77–79) aus und schreibe sie hier in Großbuchstaben auf. Zeige sie nicht deiner Partnerin / deinem Partner!*

1 _____   2 _____

b) *Buchstabiere die Wörter für deine Partnerin oder deinen Partner. Sie oder er schreibt sie auf. Dann schreibe die Wörter auf, die deine Partnerin oder dein Partner dir buchstabiert.*

1 _____   2 _____

c) *Überprüfe, ob du deine Wörter richtig geschrieben hast.*

---

[1] **first name** *Vorname*   [2] **family name** *Familienname*   [3] **address** *Adresse*   [4] **road** *Straße*

Digital quiz   **Ich kann Wörter richtig buchstabieren.**

Present your dream room

Step 1

▶ Digital help

Schau dir das Poster an und überlege wie dein Traumzimmer aussehen könnte.

There's a ...
cat • chair • computer • desk •
dog • games console[1] • lamp •
small / big / black / red / ... sofa •
TV • wardrobe • ...

There are ...
books • clothes • comics • a lot of
posters • ...

▶ Wordbank 9, p. 175

Step 2

Fertige ein Poster von deinem Traumzimmer an. Male Bilder oder finde passende Fotos und schneide sie aus. Schreibe ein paar Sätze dazu.

My dream room

There's a big red sofa. There's a black cat on my bed.
There are three computers. There are a lot of comics.

Step 3

Stelle dein Traumzimmer deiner Gruppe vor. Lies den Text und zeige dein Poster.

[1] **games console** *Spielekonsole*

tal quiz

Ich kann mein Traumzimmer präsentieren.

1 Words **Jay's favourite picture**

Ich kann **über meine Familie sprechen.**

Complete the sentences.
Write the family words.
Ergänze die Sätze.
Schreibe die Familienwörter auf.

This is my family.

My m*um* and my

d*ad* are behind the sofa.

My s*ister* and g*randpa* are next to me.

Meera is my a*unt* . Sunita and Nish are my c*ousins* .

2 **On the phone with *FindAPet***

Ich kann **über Tiere sprechen.**

a) Language **Lily is on the phone with Mrs Taylor from *FindAPet*. Complete Mrs Taylor's questions with *is* or *are*.** *Lily telefoniert mit Frau Taylor von FindAPet. Ergänze Frau Taylors Fragen mit* is *oder* are.

Mrs Taylor

Lily

b) **Answer the questions for you.** (Circle) **the right answer.**
Beantworte die Fragen für dich. Umkreise die richtige Antwort.

You

	Lily	You
1 *Are* you good with animals?	Yes, I am.	Yes, I am. / No, I'm not.
2 *Is* your home big?	No, it isn't.	Yes, it is. / No, it isn't.
3 *Is* your home quiet?	Yes, it is.	Yes, it is. / No, it isn't.
4 *Are* you and your family cat fans?	No, we aren't.	Yes, we are. / No, we aren't.
5 *Are* your neighbours dog fans?	No, they aren't.	Yes, they are. / No, they aren't.

c) **Ask your partner questions from a). She or he answers. Take turns.**
Stellt euch zu zweit die Fragen aus a) und beantwortet sie. Wechselt euch ab.

Check

◀) **3** Listening **Noah's room**
1.41

a) **Listen to Noah.** (Circle) **the things in his room.**
Höre Noah zu. Kreise die Dinge in seinem Zimmer ein.

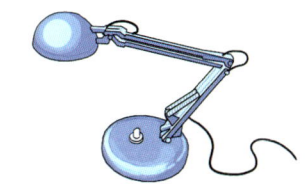  

b) **Listen again. Tick (✓) the right answer.**
Höre noch einmal zu. Mache ein Häkchen (✓) hinter die richtige Antwort.

1	Is Noah's room tidy?	Yes, it is.	✓	No, it isn't.	☐
2	Where is Noah's desk?	In front of the shelves.	✓	Behind the shelves.	☐
3	Where is Buddy?	In the bed.	☐	Under the bed.	✓
4	Is Noah's room quiet?	Yes, it is.	✓	No, it isn't.	☐

◀) **4** Listening **At the vet**
1.42

There are two new animals at the vet. Listen and complete the information.
Es gibt zwei neue Tiere bei der Tierärztin. Höre zu und ergänze die Information.

1
Pet's name: Queenie
Animal: hamster
Family name: F R U I N
Phone number: 4960 1 6 2

2
Pet's name: Hermes
Animal: parrot
Family name: L U I
Phone number: 07700 9 0 0 8 3 5

Check ⬇

VARNDEAN
Teen Zine

Our school magazine

Lucy's poems[1]

Here are two poems about pets. You can write a pet poem too!

★
> I have a dog
> He has a blog
> He's always fine
> When he's online!

★
> I have a snake
> His name is Jake
> He's white and green
> And very mean!

My pet by Max

I have a bearded dragon[2] or a 'beardie'.
His name is Drago and he's grey and
yellow. He's four.

Beardies can swim fast.
They live for 10–12 years.

Drago has a big terrarium with a lamp.
It's warm under the lamp.

I think a bearded dragon is a great pet!

Hello!

We think Drago is cool! What about you?
Is your pet great? Write to us and send a photo!

---

[1] **poem** *Gedicht*   [2] **bearded dragon** *Bartagame (Echsenart)*

Puzzle time

Where do they live?

Emma, Zendaya, Leon und Danny all live in the same street[1]. But in which houses?
Write the names under the right houses.

- Emma's house number isn't 2 or 6.
- Emma and Danny live at the beginning and end of the street.
- Zendaya's house is between[2] Emma's house and Leon's house.
- Leon's house is next to Danny's house.

Danny   *Leon*   *Zendaya*   *Emma*

Make a paper family

You need:

- a piece of paper (DIN A4)
- a pencil
- scissors[3]
- coloured pens

1
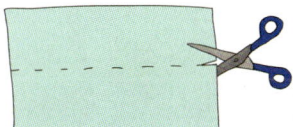

Fold[4] an A4 piece of paper in half. Cut[5] it in two.

2
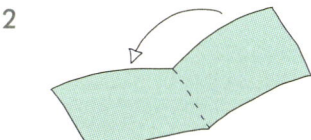

Take one piece. Fold it in half.

3

Fold it in half again.

4
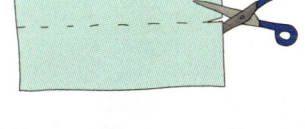

Draw a person on one side of the folded paper.

5

Cut out the person.

6

Open the paper. You can draw on the paper.

---

[1] **street** *Straße*   [2] **between** *zwischen*   [3] **scissors** *Schere*   [4] **fold** *falten*   [5] **cut** *schneiden*

Teen Zine special: Festivals

Christmas

I'm Lyle and this is my sister Astra.
This is how we celebrate[1] Christmas in my family.

Before Christmas

★ We decorate the tree.
★ My friends and I go to the neighbours' houses and sing Christmas songs.

Christmas Eve[2] (24th December)

★ We hang up[3] our stockings.
★ We make Christmas cookies.
★ We put cookies and milk under the tree for Father Christmas and a carrot for reindeer Rudolph.

Christmas Day (25th December)

★ We open our presents[4].
★ We eat turkey for dinner.
★ My grandparents and cousins eat dinner with us.
★ After dinner we play games.

---

[1] **celebrate** *feiern*   [2] **Eve** *Vorabend*   [3] **hang up** *aufhängen*   [4] **present** *Geschenk*

Chinese New Year

I'm Vivian.
My family is Chinese and we live in Brighton.
Chinese New Year is in January or February.
There are big parties for Chinese New Year in Brighton.

There are 15 days of Chinese New Year celebrations[1].

Day 1:___ We visit[2] old people.
Day 2:___ Today is a special day for dogs.
Day 3:___ This is a quiet day.
Day 4:___ We make meals[3] for the week.
Day 5:___ We clean[4] the house.
Day 6:___ We throw away[5] old things.
Day 12:___ We get ready[6] for the Lantern Festival.
Day 13:___ We eat vegetarian meals.

---

[1] **celebration** *Feier*   [2] **visit** *besuchen*   [3] **meal** *Mahlzeit*   [4] **clean** *putzen*
[5] **throw away** *wegwerfen*   [6] **get ready** *sich vorbereiten*

► page 49

Extra practice 1

Complete the table. Use the words from the box.

Ergänze die Tabelle. Verwende die Wörter aus dem Kasten.

> ~~aunt~~ • ~~brother~~ • ~~cousin~~ • dad • grandma • grandpa •
> mum • partner • sister • uncle

🧍	🧍‍♀️	🧍 or 🧍‍♀️
brother	aunt	cousin
dad	grandma	partner
grandpa	mum	
uncle	sister	

► page 51

Extra practice 2

Make questions about Scout's family with *is* or *are*.

Bilde Fragen über Scouts Familie mit is *oder* are.

1 <u>Is</u> Sally Scout's cousin?

2 <u>Are</u> Scout's mum and dad from Brighton?

3 <u>Are</u> Scout's brothers very loud?

4 <u>Is</u> Sally very friendly?

5 <u>Is</u> Scout's mum happy?

I **am**
you **are**
he/she/it **is**
we **are**
they **are**

Extra practice 3 ▸ page 53

a) **Look at the animals. What do you think? Tick (✓) the words that describe them.**
Schau dir die Tiere an. Was denkst du? Hake (✓) die Wörter ab, die sie beschreiben.

1

This dog is ...

big. ☐

friendly. ☐

old. ☐

cute. ☐

2

This monkey is ...

fast. ☐

cute. ☐

quiet. ☐

slow. ☐

3

This elephant is ...

fast. ☐

mean. ☐

small. ☐

loud. ☐

4

This snake is ...

slow. ☐

mean. ☐

loud. ☐

cute. ☐

b) **Check your answers with a partner. Do you think the same?** *Vergleiche deine Antworten mit einer Partnerin oder einem Partner. Denkt ihr das Gleiche?*

▶ page 55

Extra practice 4

a) **Partner A: Choose a picture – don't tell your partner! Talk about the home.**
Partner A: Suche dir ein Bild aus – sage deiner Partnerin oder deinem Partner nicht, welches! Sprich über das Haus.

There's	a big house.	a red door.
	a small house.	a garden.
	an old house.	a balcony.
There are	a lot of trees.	
	two windows.	
	no trees.	
	a lot of balconies.	

Partner B: Guess the picture. *Partner B: Errate das Bild.*

> It's picture 1 / 2 / …

b) **Partner B: Choose a different picture and talk about it.**
Partner B: Wähle ein anderes Bild und sprich darüber.

Partner A: Guess the picture. *Partner A: Errate das Bild.*

▶ page 56

Extra practice 5

Help Nish. Complete his homework about his room.
Write the words. *Hilf Nish. Ergänze seine Hausaufgabe über*
sein Zimmer. Schreibe die fehlenden Wörter auf.

shelf – shelves!

In my room there's a big *bed* _____  .

There's a nice blue *wardrobe* _____ with my *clothes* _____  .

There's a big *desk* _____  and a *chair* _____ .

There are brown *shelves* _____ 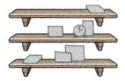 with *books* _____  .

There are three *lamps* _____ .

▶ page 58

Extra practice 6

Say where the things or animals are. Your partner says the
thing or animal. Take turns. *Beschreibe, wo die Sachen*
oder die Tiere sind. Deine Partnerin oder dein Partner errät
die Sache oder das Tier. Wechselt euch ab.

- in – *in*
- on – *auf*
- under – *unter*
- behind – *hinter*
- in front of – *vor*
- next to – *neben*

It's under the desk.

It's a rabbit.

▶ page 59

Extra practice 7

a) ~~Cross out~~ the wrong word in each answer and write the correct word.

Streiche das falsche Wort in jeder Antwort durch und schreibe das richtige Wort auf.

1 Who is Meera?	She's Sunita's ~~aunt~~.	*mum*
2 What colour is the sofa in Sunita's bedroom?	It's ~~yellow~~.	*red*
3 Where is the computer in Sunita's bedroom?	It's on the ~~bed~~.	*desk*
4 What colour is the lamp in Sunita's bedroom?	It's ~~green~~.	*yellow*
5 Who is Ben?	He's Meera's ~~uncle~~.	*partner*

b) Ask a partner the questions in a). Check the answers. Take turns.

Stelle einer Partnerin oder einem Partner die Fragen in a). Vergleicht die Antworten. Wechselt euch ab.

Extra practice 8

▶ page 59

Read the questions and answers. Write who, what or where in the questions.

Lies die Fragen und Antworten. Ergänze who, what oder where in den Fragen.

1 <u>What</u> is the name of your school? – My school's name is Varndean.

2 <u>Where</u> is your home? – It's in Hove.

3 <u>Who</u> is your teacher? – My teacher is Mrs Price.

4 <u>What</u> is your favourite thing? – It's my phone.

5 <u>What</u> is your name? – My name is Ashley.

🔊 Unit 2 – My family and home

▶ p. 48	grandpa	der Opa
	grandma	die Oma
	uncle	der Onkel
	brother	der Bruder
	aunt	die Tante
▶ p. 49	family	die Familie
	cousin	der Cousin, die Cousine
	neighbour	der Nachbar, die Nachbarin

Topic 1

▶ p. 50	Are you OK?	Geht es dir gut?
	quiet	ruhig, still, leise
	at home	zu Hause
	home	das Heim, das Zuhause
	angry	wütend
	vet	der Tierarzt, die Tierärztin
	weekend	das Wochenende
	a lot (of)	viel/e; sehr
	work	die Arbeit
	house	das Haus
	good	gut
	too loud	zu laut
	loud	laut
	messy	unordentlich
	pet	das (Haus-)Tier
▶ p. 52	for	für
	please	bitte
▶ p. 53	slow	langsam
	fast	schnell
	cute	niedlich, süß

a vet with a dog

Topic 2

▶ p. 54	garden	der Garten
	tree	der Baum
	flat	die Wohnung
	balcony	der Balkon
	garage	die Garage

tree

a garden

there's (= there is)	es ist … / es gibt …
there are	es sind … / es gibt …
▶ p. 55 (to) **live**	leben, wohnen
living room	das Wohnzimmer
bathroom	das Bad(ezimmer)
kitchen	die Küche
bedroom	das Schlafzimmer

Topic 3

▶ p. 56 **lamp**	die Lampe
cushion	das Kissen
clothes (pl)	die Kleidung, die Kleidungsstücke
shelf, pl **shelves**	das Regal
bed	das Bett
wardrobe	der Kleiderschrank
sofa	das Sofa
robot	der Roboter
chocolate	die Schokolade
chair	der Stuhl
on	auf
▶ p. 57 **next to**	neben
in front of	vor
behind	hinter
door	die Tür
under	unter
Where …?	Wo …?
tidy	ordentlich
▶ p. 59 **he/she/it has**	er/sie/es hat

(to) have

I	have	he	has
you	have	she	has
we	have	it	has
they	have		

its terrarium	sein Terrarium / ihr Terrarium

I –	my name	we –	our names
you –	your name	you –	your names
he –	his name	they –	their names
she –	her name	it –	its name

Story

▶ p. 60 alone — allein

parents (pl) — die Eltern

at work — bei der Arbeit, am Arbeitsplatz

cook — der Koch, die Köchin

guitar — die Gitarre

(to) talk (to) — sprechen, reden (mit)

now — nun, jetzt

Bye. — Auf Wiedersehen! / Servus.

▶ p. 61 dinner — das Abendessen

bad — schlecht; schlimm

(to) play — spielen

headphones (pl) — der Kopfhörer

Is there ...? — Gibt es ...?

still — (immer) noch

problem — das Problem

all — alle(s)

game — das Spiel

back — zurück

back at home — wieder zu Hause

▶ p. 62 great — großartig, toll

about — wegen, über

message — die Nachricht, die Mitteilung

Study skills

▶ p. 64 phone number — die Telefonnummer

15 fifteen	21 twenty-one	40 forty	100 a/one hundred
16 sixteen	22 twenty-two	50 fifty	101 a/one hundred and one
17 seventeen	(...)	60 sixty	102 a/one hundred and two
18 eighteen	30 thirty	70 seventy	103 a/one hundred and three
19 nineteen	31 thirty-one	80 eighty	(...)
20 twenty	(...)	90 ninety	

▶ Numbers, p. 277

Unit task

▶ p. 65 TV — der Fernseher; das Fernsehen

Unit 3
My day

A

B

School journeys
Five students at Varndean talk about their school journeys. Three students have a long journey. Two students have a short journey. 😊 ❤️

1 Listening School journeys

a) Before you listen **Look at the photos on pages 80–81. Draw lines.**
Sieh dir die Fotos auf den Seiten 80–81 an. Ziehe Linien.

1 Zane:	I go to school by bike. 🚲
2 Sunita:	I walk to school. 🚶
3 Noah:	I go to school by bus. 🚌
4 Lily:	I go to school by car. 🚗
5 Alice:	I go to school by train. 🚄

b) Listen. Check your answers in a). *Höre zu. Überprüfe deine Antworten in a).*
2.1

Nach dieser Unit kann ich ...

- ○ über meinen Schulweg sprechen
- ○ meinen Alltag beschreiben
- ○ mich verabreden
- ○ neue Wörter nachschlagen und lernen

Unit task

- ○ die Höhepunkte meiner Woche vorstellen

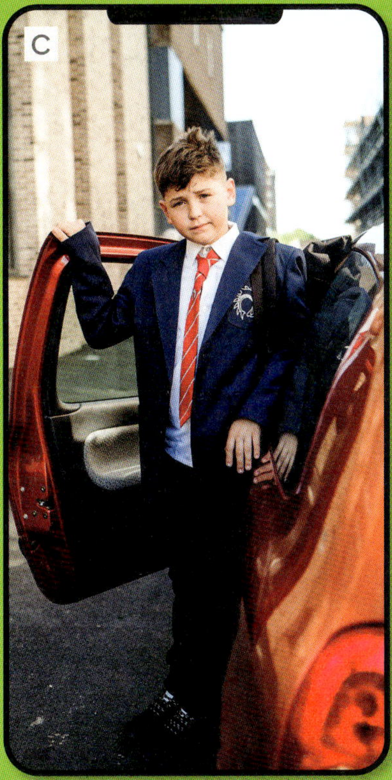

C

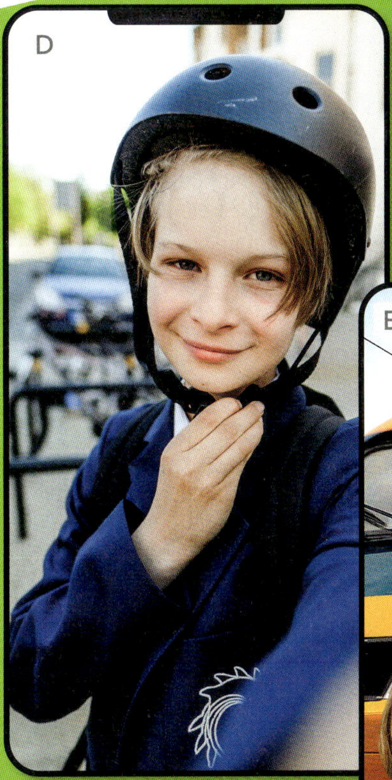

D

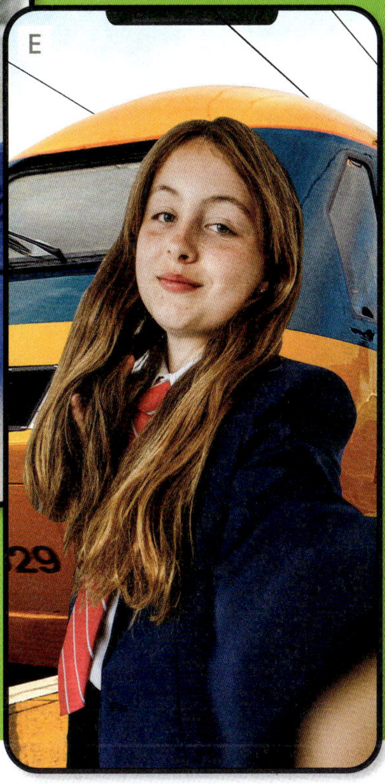

E

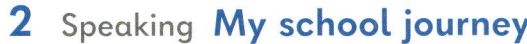

2 Speaking **My school journey**

Walk around **Talk about your school journey. Find three students with the same transport.** *Sprich über deinen Schulweg. Finde drei Kinder mit dem gleichen Schulweg.*

I go to school by bus. What about you?
I go to school by bike.

▸ Extra practice 1–2, p. 100

tal quiz **Ich kann über meinen Schulweg sprechen.** ✓

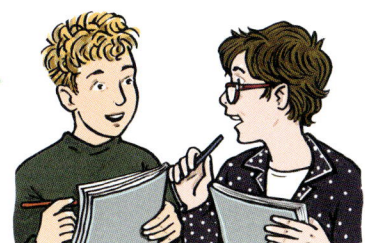

A weekday

1 Words **Big numbers**

🔊 2.2

a) *Höre zu und wiederhole die Zahlen. Stehe auf, wenn du die blauen Zahlen hörst. Setze dich hin, wenn du die schwarzen Zahlen hörst.*

| 10 | 15 | 20 | 25 | 30 | 35 | 40 | 45 | 50 | 55 | 60 |

🔊 2.3

b) *Höre dir die Zahlen an. Wenn die Zahl kleiner ist als 20, mache dich klein.*
Wenn die Zahl größer ist als 20, mache dich groß.

▶ Extra practice 3, p. 101

2 Listening **It's time for ...**

🔊 2.4

a) **Before you listen** **Look at the box with times.**
Listen and clap the rhythm. *Schau dir die Box mit den Uhrzeiten an. Höre zu und klatsche den Rhythmus.*

> 8.00 = eight o'clock
> 8.05 = eight oh five
> 8.10 = eight ten

| a 8 o'clock | b 8.05 | c 8.10 | d 8.15 | e 8.20 | f 8.25 |
| g 8.30 | h 8.35 | i 8.40 | j 8.45 | k 8.50 | l 8.55 | m 9 o'clock |

b) **Write the times.** *Schreibe die Uhrzeiten auf.*

What's the time?

> 3.05 • 2.30 • 4.50 • 4.15 • 3.45 • 9.00

1 It's four fifteen. *4.15*   2 It's three forty-five. *3.45*   3 It's four fifty. *4.50*

4 It's two thirty. *2.30*   5 It's three oh five. *3.05*   6 It's nine o'clock. *9.00*

🔊 2.5

c) **Listen.** (Circle) **the right time.** *Höre zu. Umkreise die richtigen Uhrzeiten.*

1 School starts at: 7.45 (8.45)   3 Lunchtime: 12.35 (12.45)

2 Lesson 1: (9.05) 9.15   4 The end of school: (3.05) 3.25

▶ Extra practice 4, p. 101

3 Speaking **The time**

Partner A: Go to page 101. *Gehe zur Seite 101.*
Partner B: Go to page 102. *Gehe zur Seite 102.*

▶ Wordbank 10, p. 176

4   Reading **Before and after school**

a) Before you read *Was trifft auf Zane zu? Arbeitet zu zweit. Mache ein Häkchen (✓) bei den richtigen Antworten.*

1 *(page 19)* His hobby is swimming. ☑   3 *(page 30)* He's always busy. ☑

2 *(page 19)* Zane likes cooking. ☑   4 *(page 31)* His dog's name is Buddy. ☐

b) Read the text. *Lies den Text.*

2.7

My son is the best!

This text for our 'Best Kids Competition[1]' is from Louise Adebayo. It's about her son Zane (11).

1 **I use a wheelchair**. My husband[2] Eno has a cafe and **he works long days**. On weekdays, my son Zane helps me.

5 Zane gets up at 7 o'clock and has a shower. He has a little sister, Holly. **She gets up at 7.30**. Eno makes breakfast for us and **we all eat breakfast**. Zane walks with his sister
10 Holly to her school at 8.15 and then he goes to his school. Then I work on the computer. I write books.

Zane meets Holly at her school at 3.20 and **they walk home**. Then he

15 does his homework. **It takes an hour**. Sometimes Zane helps me with dinner.

Or he talks with his friends or watches TV. On Friday he goes swimming.

20 Zane, **you help me a lot**. You're the best!

c) Put the activities in the right order. Write 1–4.
Bringe die Aktivitäten in die richtige Reihenfolge. Schreibe 1–4.

a __2__ Holly gets up at 7.30.

b __3__ Zane walks with his sister Holly to her school at 8.15.

c __1__ Zane gets up at 7 o'clock.

d __4__ Zane meets Holly at her school at 3.20.   ▸ Extra practice 5, p. 102

---

[1] **Best Kids Competition** *Wettbewerb für die besten Kinder*   [2] **husband** *Ehemann*

Erklär-film

5 Looking at language **Simple present**

a) **Complete the sentences from the text.** *Ergänze die Sätze aus dem Text.*

1 I _use_ a wheelchair. (*Zeile 1*)

2 You _help_ me a lot. (*Zeile 20*)

3 We all _eat_ breakfast. (*Zeile 8–9*)

4 They _walk_ home. (*Zeile 14*)

5 He _works_ long days. (*Zeile 2–3*)

6 She _gets_ up at 7.30. (*Zeile 7*)

7 It _takes_ an hour. (*Zeile 15*)

b) *Sieh dir die eingesetzten Wörter rechts in* a) *an. Wie unterscheiden sie sich von den Wörtern links? Umkreise den letzten Buchstaben.*

c) *Umkreise die richtige Antwort. Wann endet das Verb auf -s? Bei* A *der* B*?*

A I / you / we / they

B he / she / it

Bei regelmäßigen Tätigkeiten verwendest du das *simple present*.
Das Verb endet bei *he/she/it* auf -s.

6 On Saturday

Circle the right word. *Umkreise das richtige Wort.*

1 On Saturday Eno make / makes breakfast.
2 Then we all eat / eats breakfast.
3 Then mum is busy. She work / works.
4 Eno, Zane and Holly go to the park.
They play / plays football.

7 Game **Weekdays**

Erzählt von eurem Schultag wie im Beispiel:

Student 1 ___ I **get** up at six thirty.
Student 2 ___ She **gets** up at six thirty.
I **make** breakfast.
Student 3 ___ He **makes** breakfast.
I **go** to school.
Student 4 ___ She **goes** ...
Student 1 ___ ...

► Extra practice 6–7, pp. 102–103

8 Song **The morning song**

a) Before you listen **Draw lines from the pictures to the right words.**
Ziehe Linien von den Bildern zu den richtigen Begriffen.

A __3__	B __1__	C __2__	D __4__	E __5__

have a shower	eat your breakfast	brush your teeth	get up	go to school

🔊 2.8 **b)** **Listen to the song. What order do you hear the activities in a)? Write 1–5 in the pictures in a).** *Höre dir das Lied an. In welcher Reihenfolge hörst du die Aktivitäten in a)? Schreibe 1–5 in die Bilder.*

🔊 2.9 **c)** **Listen to the end of the song. What day is it?**
Höre dir das Ende des Liedes an. Welcher Tag ist es?

It's *Saturday* _____ .

d) **Listen again and act out the song.** *Höre noch einmal zu und spiele das Lied vor.*

▶ Extra practice 8, p. 104

My task

9 My school day

Writing **Read Zane's text. Then write a text about your day.**
Lies Zanes Text. Schreibe dann einen Text über deinen Tag.

> I get up at 7 o'clock.
> I go to school at 8.15.
> I have lunch at 12.30.
> School ends at 3.15.
> I go to bed at 9 o'clock.

▶ Digital help 🔊   ▶ Wordbank 10, p. 176

 tal quiz 🔊 **Ich kann** meinen Alltag beschreiben. ✓

School clubs

1 Listening **Sports and hobbies**

a) **Before you listen** Write the number of the picture next to the correct word.
Schreibe die Nummer des Bildes neben das richtige Wort.

A trampolining _7_ B playing computer games _8_ C running _5_ D dancing _3_

E table tennis _1_ F windsurfing _6_ G singing _4_ H cricket _2_

b) **Listen. For each person, tick (✓) the two activities they talk about.**
Höre zu. Mache für jede Person neben die zwei Aktivitäten, über die sie spricht, ein Häkchen (✓).

2.10

1 **Annie**	✓ table tennis	☐ dancing	✓ cricket
2 **Brahim**	✓ singing	✓ running	☐ playing computer games
3 **Rin**	☐ table tennis	✓ windsurfing	✓ dancing
4 **Liam**	✓ trampolining	☐ cricket	✓ computer games

c) **Talk to your partner about the activities. Use the words in a) or use your own ideas.**
Sprecht zu zweit über die Aktivitäten. Benutzt die Wörter in a) oder findet eigene Ideen.

> *I like singing. What about you?*

> *I like dancing and football.*

2 How often?

2.10

a) Listen again. (Circle) the right words.

Höre noch einmal zu. Umkreise die richtigen Wörter.

1 Annie sometimes / (often) plays table tennis.

2 Brahim sometimes / (never) goes running.

3 Rin (sometimes) / never does dancing.

4 Liam often / (rarely) plays computer games.

b) **Put the words in the correct order.** *Setze die Wörter in die richtige Reihenfolge.*

sometimes • often • ~~never~~ • always • rarely

never	rarely	sometimes	often	always
nie	selten	manchmal	oft	immer

▶ Extra practice 9–10, pp. 104–105

3 Speaking **Surfing sentences**

Seht euch das Bild zu zweit an. Macht wahre Sätze über euch.

I often go surfing.

often
sometimes
I
never
rarely

play
go

football.
cycling.
surfing.
hockey.
swimming.

4 Mediation **A very special school club**

a) *Lies das Poster über eine Schul-AG der Varndean Schule. Arbeitet zu zweit.*

Partner/in A: Du verstehst das Poster nicht. Stelle Partner/in B die Fragen 1–3.
Partner/in B: Beantworte die Fragen auf Deutsch.

1 Was baut man in dieser AG? <u>elektrische Autos aus (alten Materialien)</u>

2 Arbeiten die Schüler/innen allein oder haben sie Hilfe? <u>Sie haben Hilfe.</u>

3 Kostet die Teilnahme etwas? <u>nein</u>

b) *Tauscht die Rollen.*

Partner/in B: Du verstehst das Poster nicht. Stelle Partner/in A die Fragen 1–3.
Partner/in A: Beantworte die Fragen auf Deutsch.

1 Welche Eigenschaften sollte man für die AG haben?
<u>aktiv sein und gut im Team</u>

2 Wann findet die AG statt? <u>freitags um 3.30 Uhr</u>

3 Wer hilft das Auto zusammenzubauen? <u>Herr Price und Frau Haffar</u>

FORMULA 24 CLUB

Are you active and good in a team?

Join the Formular 24 Club!

We make an electric car from old materials.

Then we race with 700 other teams.

We meet every Friday at 3.30.

Mr Price and Mrs Haffar help us make the car.

The club is free!

5 Speaking **Secret sentences**

a) *Schreibe drei Sätze über dich mit* always, often, sometimes *oder* never *auf. Ein Satz ist wahr, zwei sind falsch. Lies die Sätze vor. Deine Partnerin oder dein Partner sagt, welcher Satz richtig ist.*

I never go swimming.

I sometimes eat chocolate.

I always play computer games.

Right!

Wrong!

Wrong!

1 (I always eat pizza on Friday.) _____

2 (I never play tennis.) _____

3 (I often help my mum.) _____

b) *Tauscht die Rollen.*

My task

6 My free time

Read the message from Annie. Write to her and answer her questions.
Write four sentences. *Lies die Nachricht von Annie. Schreibe ihr und beantworte ihre Fragen. Schreibe vier Sätze.*

Hi, I'm Annie.
I want an online friend.
What activities do you do and how often?
What are your hobbies? ✓

Hi, I'm (Shamim. I sometimes play football. I never play table tennis.

I like dancing but I don't like cycling. My favourite hobby is swimming.)

_____

▶ Digital help    ▶ Wordbank 4, p. 171

Meeting friends

1 Reading Are you busy?

a) **Read the messages. Which two people are writing?**
Lies die Nachrichten. Welche zwei Personen schreiben einander?

Zane   and *Lily*

b) **Write *Zane* or *Lily*.**
Schreibe Zane oder Lily.

1 *Lily*   wants to meet at the weekend.

2 *Zane*   is busy at the weekend.

3 *Zane*   says sorry.

4 *Lily*   is sad.

> Hi, Zane, are you free on Saturday?
>
> Sorry, Lily. I'm busy on Saturday.
>
> Oh, OK. Let's meet on Sunday.
>
> Sorry, I can't. On Sunday I have a swimming competition.
>
> Oh, OK. You're always busy, Zane! ☹

2 Listening Let's meet

a) **Before you listen Write the phrases in the right place.**
Schreibe die Redewendungen an die richtige Stelle.

Sorry, I'm busy. •
Yes, please! •
Can we meet …? •
Let's … •
I'd love to. •
Sorry, I can't.

Ask to meet	Say yes 🙂	Say no ☹
Let's …	*I'd love to.*	*Sorry, I'm busy.*
Can we meet …?	*Yes, please!*	*Sorry, I can't.*

b) **Listen. When do Lily and Noah meet?**
Höre zu. Wann treffen sich Lily und Noah?

Lily and Noah meet at *10.30*   (Uhrzeit)

on *Sunday*   (Tag).

▶ Extra practice 11, p. 105

3 Role-play **Can we meet this weekend?**

Go to page 106. Read Lily's and Noah's conversation. Then act it out.
Geht zur Seite 106. Lest Lilys und Noahs Gespräch. Spielt es vor.

▶ Extra practice 12, p. 106

My task

4 Are you free?

a) *Diesen Kalender brauchst du zum Ausfüllen für c).*

Saturday	Sunday
Activity: _____	Activity: *(go to the beach)* _____
With: _____	With: *(Lena)* _____
Activity: _____	Activity: _____
With: _____	With: _____

b) Double circle *Stellt euch in zwei Kreisen auf. Wähle eine Aktivität. Schlage sie deinem Gegenüber im Kreis vor. Nenne einen Tag. Dein Gegenüber antwortet. Ein Kreis bewegt sich nach links. Seht euch den Beispieldialog und das Bild an.*

> go to the beach • go to the park • go to the skatepark •
> go swimming • go cycling • meet at my house/flat • play football

Let's go to the beach.

Good idea!

Are you free on Saturday?

No, sorry. Can we meet on Sunday?

Yes, please!

c) *Schreibe in deinen Kalender in a), wenn ihr euch auf einen Termin und eine Aktivität einigen konntet. Redet mit anderen Kindern.*

The competition

1 Reading **About the story**

a) **Before you read** **Look at the title and the pictures.** (Circle) A, B or C.
Sieh dir die Überschrift und die Bilder an. Umkreise A, B oder C.

A Zane isn't the winner of the competition.
B Zane is the winner. His friends are really happy for him.
C Zane is the winner. His friends are angry at him.

b) **Read the story and check your answer from a).**
Lies die Geschichte und überprüfe deine Antwort in a).

2.12

1

"Look, Lily! It's Zane!" Lily's mum says.
Lily looks at the newspaper[1].
"What?" Lily is really surprised.
"Zane's mum is in a wheelchair?"
She takes a photo of the newspaper
and tells Sunita and Noah.

2

After school, Lily, Sunita and Noah talk to Zane.
"Hi Zane," Sunita says. "We know about your mum. But why is it a secret?"
"I'm sad because it's hard for her," says Zane.
"So I often help at home. But I don't like to talk about it."

3

"Zane, you help your mum – that's cool," says Lily. "But we're your friends. You can tell us."
"Don't be angry, Lily," says Zane.
"People see mum in her wheelchair and they are sorry[2] for her. But please don't be sorry for her – she's great. And don't be sorry for me!"

---

[1] **newspaper** *Zeitung*   [2] **be sorry for** *Mitleid haben mit*

🔊
2.13

4

Later at Zane's home, Zane's mum is on the phone.

"Hello, Louise Adebayo. Really? Thank you! Bye."

"Zane! You're the *Best Kids Competition* winner!" His mum is happy.

"Thanks, Mum," says Zane. "I love you!"

5

Zane tells his friends. Everybody is happy! But Zane's mum is tired and she is in bed for two days.

"The prize show isn't a good idea, Mum."

"Why not? I can do it."

"OK, Mum!" Zane says.

6

At the prize show ...

"Thank you! I'm so happy. Mum and Dad and Holly – you're the best! And thanks to my friends Lily, Sunita and Noah!

There's some prize money for the winner. I'd like to ..."

---

2 Headings

In which parts can you find these sentences? Write 1–6.

In welchen Abschnitten findest du diese Sätze? Schreibe 1–6.

a Zane: "Thank you. I'm so happy." _____6_____

b Sunita: "We know about your mum." _____2_____

c Lily: "Zane's mum is in a wheelchair?" _____1_____

d Zane's mum: "I can do it." _____5_____

e Lily: "We're your friends." _____3_____

f Zane's mum: "You're the *Best Kids Competition* winner!" _____4_____

3   Who is it?

(Circle) the right name. *Umkreise den richtigen Namen.*

1 (Lily) / Sunita takes a photo of the newspaper.

2 Lily / (Sunita) asks Zane about his secret.

3 Noah / (Zane) tells his friends about his mum.

4   Showtime **Freeze!**

a) *Wie fühlen sich die Kinder in den Abschnitten 1,2,4 und 5? Schreibe die richtigen Wörter.*

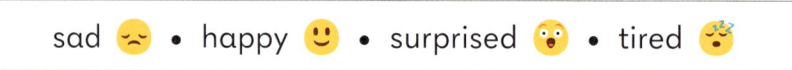

sad 😔 • happy 🙂 • surprised 😲 • tired 😴

Part 1: Lily is *surprised* .

Part 4: Zane's mum is *happy* .

Part 2: Zane is *sad* about his mum.

Part 5: Zane's mum is *tired* .

b) *Wähle einen Abschnitt aus der Geschichte. Führe ein passendes Standbild vor. Benutze dabei deinen ganzen Körper und dein Gesicht. Die Klasse sagt, welchen Abschnitt du vorführst.*

It's part 5. Zane's friends are happy.

5   Zane's prize money

a) *Zane gewinnt £500. Wie viele Euro sind das? Recherchiere im Internet.*

£500 is *(576)* Euro.

b) *Was macht Zane mit dem Geld? Ratet gemeinsam. Nutzt die Ideen unten oder andere.*

- He gets a new video console.
- He has a big party.
- He gives some money to his mum and dad.
- He gets a new TV for his family.

I think he …   *Yes, I think you're right.*   *No, I don't think so.*

c) **Listen to Zane's ideas. Are they the same as yours?**
Hört Zane zu. Hattet ihr die gleichen Ideen?

Digital quiz 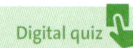   **Ich kann** Gefühle in einer Geschichte verstehen.   ✓

The Brighton dares: Sports and hobbies

1 About Daisy and Emir

Before you watch Look at the lists. What are Daisy's and Emir's hobbies? *Sieh dir die Listen an. Was sind Daisys und Emirs Hobbys?*

Emir
do drama
play football

Daisy
play table tennis
go swimming

Daisy plays table tennis and she ...

---

2 Viewing **Time for a new dare**

Watch the video. (Circle) the correct picture (A or B) for each dare.
Sieh dir das Video an. Umkreise das richtige Bild (A oder B) für jede Mutprobe.

Daisy's dare[1] for Emir:

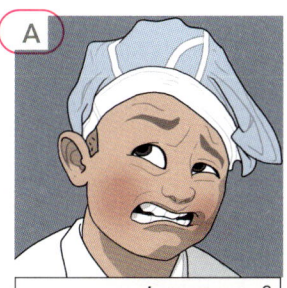

A wear underpants[2] on his head

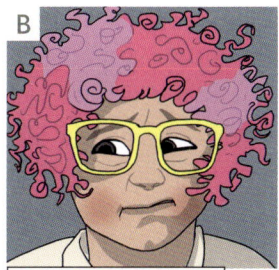

B wear pink hair

Emir's dare for Daisy:

A make a street drawing

B play street music

---

3 Viewing **Who helps? Who can't help?**

a) Can you remember? Match. Then watch again and check. *Erinnert ihr euch? Ordnet zu. Seht euch das Video dann noch einmal an und überprüft.*

1	Gloria helps Emir.		She has a trip to London.
2	Amal can't help Daisy.		She can't play for six weeks.
3	Gloria can't help Daisy.		She gives him a good idea.

b) What do Emir and Daisy do? Complete the sentences. *Was machen Emir und Daisy? Ergänze die Sätze.*

1 Emir makes a beanie[3] from u*nderpants* . 2 Daisy plays the air[4] g*uitar* .

---

[1] **dare** *Mutprobe*   [2] **underpants** *Unterhose*   [3] **beanie** *Mütze*   [4] **air** *Luft*

Look up and remember words

1 Look up free-time activities

Look at Wordbank 4 on page 171. Write the activities in English.
Sieh dir die Wordbank 4 auf Seite 171 an. Schreibe die Aktivitäten auf Englisch.

Backen: _b_ a _k_ i _n_ _g_

Boxen: b _o_ _x_ i _n_ _g_

Kajakfahren: _k_ a _y_ a k _i_ _n_ _g_

Reiten: h _o_ _r_ _s_ e r _i_ _d_ i _n_ _g_

2 Odd word out

Circle the odd word out. *Umkreise das Wort, das nicht passt.*

1 running	swimming	cycling	(drawing)
2 (cola)	burger	sandwich	fish
3 book	(money)	exercise	page
4 kitchen	bathroom	(sofa)	living room
5 old	big	quiet	(house)

Digital quiz **Ich kann** neue Wörter nachschlagen und lernen.

Share your highlights of the week

Step 1

Write three sentences about the best things you do every week.
Schreibe drei Sätze über die besten Sachen, die du jede Woche tust.

Example: On Wednesday I have a singing lesson.

On Saturday I always get up at 10 o'clock.

On Sunday I often play football with my sister.

(On Friday I play football.

On Saturday I play computer games.

On Sunday I watch videos.)

▶ Wordbank 4, p. 171

Step 2

You choose Do task A or B. *Mache Task A oder Task B.*

Task A	Task B
Male deine Aktivitäten aus *Step 1* wie einen Comic. Schreibe deine Sätze unter deinen Comic. Zeige der Klasse deinen Comic. 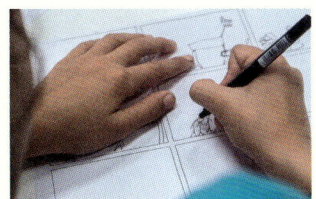	Mache ein Video mit deinem Handy. Lies deine Sätze aus *Step 1* vor und zeige passende Gegenstände. Zeige der Klasse dein Video. 

Step 3

Look at the comics and watch the videos. Give feedback.
Seht euch die Comics und Videos an. Gebt Feedback.

Your comic is cool!   *Your video is very nice.*

 **Ich kann** die Höhepunkte meiner Woche vorstellen.

1 Reading Zara's school journey

 Ich kann über meinen Schulweg sprechen.

a) Read the email from Zane's friend Zara. *Lies die E-Mail von Zanes Freundin Zara.*

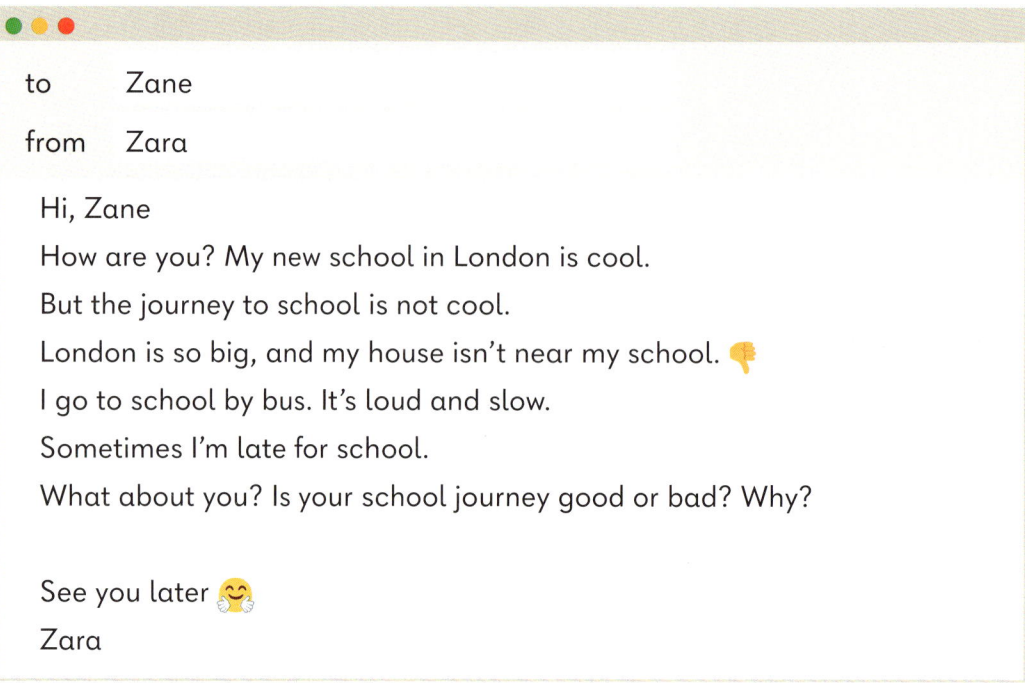

to   Zane

from   Zara

Hi, Zane

How are you? My new school in London is cool.

But the journey to school is not cool.

London is so big, and my house isn't near my school. 👎

I go to school by bus. It's loud and slow.

Sometimes I'm late for school.

What about you? Is your school journey good or bad? Why?

See you later 🤗

Zara

b) Read the sentences. True (✓) or false (✗)?
Lies die Sätze. Richtig (✓) oder falsch (✗)?

1 Zara's school is in Brighton. ✗

2 She's happy at her school. ✓

3 Her house is near her school. ✗

4 The bus is quiet. ✗

5 She's sometimes late for school. ✓

c) Speaking Talk about your school journey with a partner.
Sprecht zu zweit über eure Schulwege.

I go to school by 🚗 / 🚲 / 🚄 / 🚌 / I 🚶 to school.

My school journey is 👍 / 👎.

My school journey is long / short.

My school journey is fast / slow.

Check

2 Words **Sunita's morning**

Ich kann meinen Alltag beschreiben. ✓

Complete the sentences with the words from the box.
Ergänze die Sätze mit den Wörtern aus der Box.

teeth • school • ~~get up~~ • shower • breakfast

I *get up* at 6.15. I have a *shower* . I brush my *teeth* .

I have my *breakfast* . I go to *school* .

3 Words **Next weekend**

Ich kann mich verabreden. ✓

Lily and Alice are talking about the weekend. Choose the right ending for each sentence. Draw lines. *Lily und Alice sprechen über das Wochenende.*
Wähle das richtige Ende für jeden Satz. Ziehe Linien.

Lily	Are you free on ...	a	busy.
Alice	Sorry, Lily. I'm ...	b	11 o'clock.
	What about Sunday? Are you ...	c	cycling.
Lily	Yes, I ...	d	Saturday?
Alice	Cool. Let's go ...	e	idea!
Lily	Good ...	f	am.
Alice	Let's meet at ...	g	free?

Check

Extra practice 1 ▶ page 81

a) (Circle) the school journey words in the word snake. *Kreise die Wörter in der Wortschlange ein, die etwas mit einem Schulweg zu tun haben.*

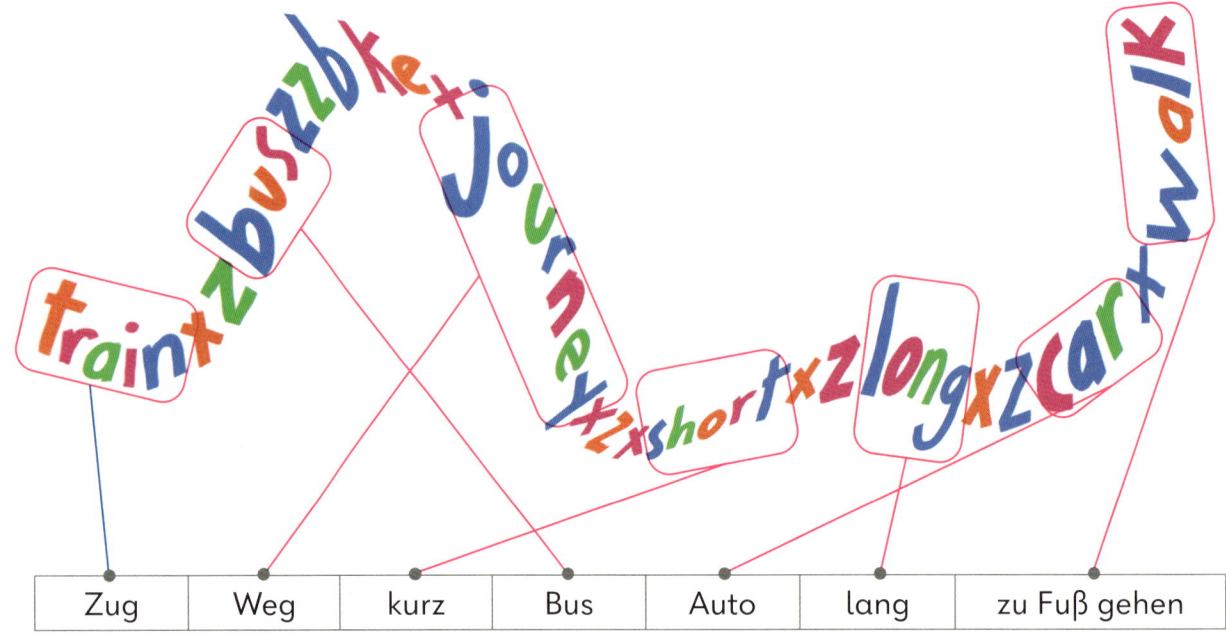

| Zug | Weg | kurz | Bus | Auto | lang | zu Fuß gehen |

b) Draw lines from the English words in the snake to the correct German words.
Ziehe Linien von den englischen Wörtern in der Schlange zu den deutschen Wörtern.

Extra practice 2 ▶ page 81

a) Look at the pictures and complete the sentences.
Sieh dir die Bilder an und ergänze die Sätze.

1   I go to school by _*bike*_ .

2   I _*walk*_ to school.

3   I go to school by _*train*_ .

4   I go to school by _*car*_ .

5   I *go to school by bus* .

b) And you? How do you go to school?
Write a sentence.
Und du? Wie gehst du zur Schule?
Schreibe einen Satz.

I *(go to school by car)* .

Extra practice 3   ▶ page 82

Write the numbers. *Schreibe die Zahlen.*

a twenty   20

b fifteen   15

c ten   10

d forty-five   45

e fifty   50

f thirty-five 35

g forty   40

h fifty-five   55

Extra practice 4   ▶ page 82

🔊
2.6

What's the time? Listen to five conversations. Number the times from 1–5.

Wie spät ist es? Höre die fünf Gespräche. Nummeriere die Uhrzeiten von 1–5.

a	b	c	d	e
10.55 2	3.30 4	8.50 1	4.20 5	12.40 3

3 Speaking **The time (Partner A)**   ▶ page 82

a) **Tell your partner the time. Your partner writes.**

Nenne die Uhrzeit. Dein Partner / Deine Partnerin schreibt.

It's ...

1 09.10   2 11.45   3 3.15   4 3.35   5 8.20

b) **Ask the time. Listen and write.** *Frage nach der Uhrzeit. Höre zu und schreibe.*

What's the time?

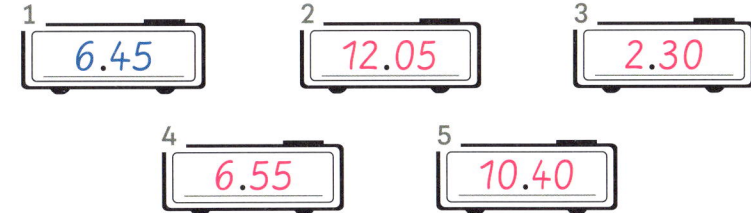

1 6.45   2 12.05   3 2.30

4 6.55   5 10.40

3 Speaking **The time (Partner B)** ▶ page 82

a) **Ask the time. Listen and write.** *Frage nach der Uhrzeit. Höre zu und schreibe.*

What's the time?

1	2	3
9.10	11.45	3.15

4	5
3.35	8.20

b) **Tell your partner the time. Your partner writes.**
Nenne die Uhrzeit. Dein Partner / Deine Partnerin schreibt.

It's ...

1	2	3	4	5
6.45	12.05	2.30	6.55	10.40

Extra practice 5 ▶ page 83

Who is it: Zane (Z), Louise (L), Eno (E) or Holly (H)? Write the letters.
Wer ist das: Zane (Z), Louise (L), Eno (E) oder Holly (H)? Schreibe die Anfangsbuchstaben ihrer Namen.

1 He watches TV. _Z_

2 She uses a wheelchair. _L_

3 She gets up at 7.30. _H_

4 He does his homework. _Z_

5 He makes breakfast. _E_

6 She goes to school with her brother. _H_

Extra practice 6 ▶ page 84

Circle the right form of the verb. *Umkreise die richtige Form des Verbs.*

1 Zane go / (goes) to swimming training.

2 He go / (goes) to the swimming pool by bike.

3 Zane and his friends has / (have) training for one hour.

4 The swimmers always (work) / works really hard.

5 Zane love / (loves) swimming.

Extra practice 7 ▶ page 84

a) **Complete the sentences about Scout's routine with the right words from the box.**
Ergänze die Sätze über Scouts Routine mit den richtigen Wörtern aus der Box.

> eat/eats • ~~get up/gets up~~ • go/goes (2x) • meet/meets • watch/watches

1
Scout always *gets up* _____ at 9 o'clock.

2
She often *goes* _____ to the beach.

3
Scout and her friend sometimes *go* _____
swimming.

4
Scout often *watches* _____ people on the beach.

5
She sometimes *eats* _____ a burger.

6
Scout and her friends often *meet* _____ .

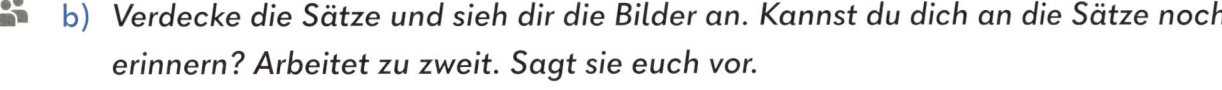

b) *Verdecke die Sätze und sieh dir die Bilder an. Kannst du dich an die Sätze noch erinnern? Arbeitet zu zweit. Sagt sie euch vor.*

Extra practice 8 ▶ page 85

a) Write the number of the correct picture (1–5).
Schreibe die Zahl des richtigen Bildes (1–5).

a I have a shower. __2__   c I go to school. __5__   e I get up. __1__

b I brush my teeth. __4__   d I eat my breakfast. __3__

b) Write about your school day. Write the activity and the time you do it.
Schreibe über deinen Schultag. Schreibe die Aktivität und die Zeit.

Example: I *get up* at *6.15* .

1 I *get up* at *(6.15)* .

2 I *have a shower* at *(6.20)* .

3 I *eat (my) breakfast* at *(6.30)* .

4 I *brush my teeth* at *(6.45)* .

5 I *go to school* at *(7.00)* .

Extra practice 9 ▶ page 87

Write the words in the correct order.
Schreibe die Wörter in der richtigen Reihenfolge.

1 never / breakfast / I / eat

   I never eat breakfast.

2 football / sometimes / play / I

   I sometimes play football.

3 cooks / My dad / always / dinner

   My dad always cooks dinner.

Extra practice 10 ▶ page 87

a) **Make the sentences true for you. Use the words in the box.**
Schreibe wahre Sätze über dich. Benutze die Wörter in der Box.

> never • rarely • sometimes • often • always

1 I *(always)* _____ play football at the weekend.

2 My English teacher *(never)* _____ gives me homework.

3 I *(sometimes)* _____ go swimming on Sunday.

4 My teacher *(rarely)* _____ goes to school by bike.

5 I *(often)* _____ eat spaghetti.

6 I *(always)* _____ work hard at school.

b) **Write these sentences in German.** *Schreibe die Sätze auf Deutsch.*

1 My grandma never eats chocolate.

   Meine Oma isst nie Schokolade.

2 Zane always walks to school.

   Zane geht immer zu Fuß zur Schule.

3 I often play computer games.

   Ich spiele oft Computerspiele.

Extra practice 11 ▶ page 90

a) **Complete the words in the conversation.** *Ergänze die Wörter in dem Gespräch.*

Niklas Hi, Ismael. Are you f*ree* _____ on Friday?

Ismael Sorry, Niklas. I'm b*usy* _____ on Friday.

Niklas Let's m*eet* _____ on Saturday!

Ismael Sorry, I c*an't* _____ on Saturday. I go to the skatepark with my mum.

Niklas Oh, OK. You're always b*usy* _____ .

b) **Check your answers on page 90.** *Überprüfe deine Antworten auf Seite 90.*

▶ page 91

Extra practice 12

a) **Read Lily's and Noah's conversation with a partner. Then act it out.**
Lest Lilys und Noahs Gespräch zu zweit. Spielt es vor.

Lily	Hi, can we meet this weekend?
Noah	Good idea!
Lily	Let's go to the cafe.
Noah	OK. Are you free on Saturday?
Lily	No, sorry. But I'm free on Sunday.
Noah	OK, let's meet at 10.30.
Lily	See you on Sunday!

b) **Write a new dialogue. Change the blue, green and red words in a).**
Schreibe einen neuen Dialog. Ändere die blauen, grünen und roten Wörter in a).

Places: skatepark • park • beach • shopping centre • cafe
Days: Friday • Saturday • Sunday
Times: 10.30 • 4.15 • 6.30 • 9.45 • 5.00

Partner A	Hi, can we meet this weekend?
Partner B	Good idea!
Partner A	Let's go to the *(park)* .
Partner B	OK. Are you free on *(Friday)* ?
Partner A	No, sorry. But I'm free on *(Saturday)* .
Partner B	OK, let's meet at *(5.00)* .
Partner A	See you on *(Saturday)* !

c) **Practise the dialogue with a partner.** *Übt den Dialog zu zweit.*

🔊 Unit 3 – My day

▶ p. 80	their	ihr
	journey	die Reise, die Fahrt
	long	lang
	short	kurz
	(to) go by bike/car/bus/...	mit dem Fahrrad/Auto/Bus/... fahren
	bike	das Fahrrad
	(to) walk	(zu Fuß) gehen
	bus	der Bus
	car	das Auto
	train	der Zug

Topic 1

▶ p. 82	8 o'clock	8 Uhr / 20 Uhr	It's **1 o'clock** now.
	What's the time?	Wie spät ist es?	
	lunchtime	Mittagszeit	
	end	das Ende, der Schluss	

15 fifteen	21 twenty-one	40 forty	100 a/one hundred
16 sixteen	22 twenty-two	50 fifty	101 a/one hundred and one
17 seventeen	(...)	60 sixty	102 a/one hundred and two
18 eighteen	30 thirty	70 seventy	103 a/one hundred and three
19 nineteen	31 thirty-one	80 eighty	(...)
20 twenty	(...)	90 ninety	▶ Numbers, p. 168

▶ p. 83	(to) cook	kochen
	son	der Sohn
	competition	Wettbewerb
	wheelchair	der Rollstuhl
	(to) work long days	lange arbeiten, lange Arbeitstage haben
	weekday	Wochentag, Werktag
	(to) get up	aufstehen
	shower	die Dusche
	little	klein
	sister	die Schwester
	(to) make	machen, herstellen
	breakfast	das Frühstück
	us	uns
	then	dann, danach
	(to) write	schreiben
	homework	die Hausaufgabe(n)

(to) **have a shower** = (sich) duschen

	(to) **take**	**dauern,** *(Zeit)* **brauchen, in Anspruch nehmen**
	hour	die Stunde
	sometimes	manchmal
	or	oder
	(to) watch (sth.)	(sich etwas) anschauen; (etwas) beobachten
	on Friday	am Freitag
▶ p.85	**tooth,** *pl* **teeth**	der Zahn
	(to) **brush your teeth**	sich die Zähne putzen
	lunch	Mittagessen
	(to) **have lunch**	zu Mittag essen

Topic 2

▶ p.86	**trampolining**	das Trampolinspringen/-turnen
	(to) **run**	rennen, laufen
	(to) **dance**	tanzen
	table tennis	das Tischtennis
	(to) **sing**	singen
▶ p.87	**often**	oft
	never	nie, niemals
	rarely	selten
	(to) **cycle**	Rad fahren
▶ p.89	**wrong**	falsch
	(to) **want**	wollen
	activity	die Aktivität, die Tätigkeit
	(to) **do**	machen, tun

cycling =
das Radfahren

Topic 3

▶ p.90	**free**	frei; kostenlos
	can't (= cannot)	nicht können
	(to) **say**	sagen
▶ p.91	**skatepark**	der Skatepark
	idea	die Idee

Story

▶ p.92	**winner**	der Gewinner, die Gewinnerin / der Sieger, die Siegerin
	really	wirklich
	surprised	überrascht
	after school	nach der Schule

	why	warum
	secret	geheim
	because	weil
	hard	schwer, schwierig; hart
	(to) be	sein
	people *(pl)*	die Leute, die Menschen
▶ p. 93	later	später
	(to) tell	erzählen, sagen
	prize	der Preis, der Gewinn
	some	etwas, ein wenig
	money	das Geld
▶ p. 94	part (of)	der Teil (von)
	(to) get	*(sich etwas)* holen/besorgen; bekommen
	(to) give	geben, schenken

Can you **give** me the book, please?

Viewing

▶ p. 95	drama	das Schauspiel, die darstellende Kunst

Unit 4
Where I live

This is my city!

1 Viewing **This is Brighton**

a) *Wähle ein Foto aus. Sage, was du siehst. Dein Partner / Deine Partnerin errät das Foto.*
I can see ...

a beach / a building / a cinema / a skatepark / a pier / a lot of people / shops / ...

b) *Schau dir das Video an. Ordne die Orte (a–g) den Fotos (1–7) zu. Schreibe die Buchstaben in die Kästchen auf den Fotos.*

a Brighton beach   b Brighton Pier   c Duke of York's cinema   d Hove Skatepark
e Brighton Marina   f Pavilion Gardens   g North Laine

Nach dieser Unit kann ich ...

○ Informationen über Brighton verstehen
○ meine Nachbarschaft beschreiben
○ über meine Stadt oder mein Dorf sprechen
○ über Sehenswürdigkeiten und
  das Wetter reden
○ Präsentationen halten

Unit task

○ die besten Orte in meiner Umgebung
  präsentieren

c) **What can you do in these places? Read sentences a–g and match them to photos 1–7. Then watch again and check.** *Was kannst du an diesen Orten tun? Lies die Sätze a–g und ordne sie den Fotos zu. Dann schau dir das Video noch einmal an und überprüfe deine Lösungen.*

a There are cool shops here. `3`

b This is a good place for a picnic. `2`

c You can watch films here. `5`

d You can go skateboarding here. `4`

e You can eat fish and chips here. `1`

f You can go bowling here. `7`

g You can go windsurfing here. `6`

▶ Extra practice 1, p. 133

My neighbourhood

2.15

1 From Lily's window

Look at the photo and listen. You're Lily. What can you see and hear? (Circle).
There is one extra in each part. *Schau dir das Foto an und höre zu. Du bist Lily.*
Was kannst du sehen und hören? Kreise ein. In jedem Teil gibt es eine Lösung zu viel.

2 Reading Lily's homework

a) **Read Lily's text. Tick (✓) the things she likes 😊 in her neighbourhood.**
Lies Lilys Text. Hake die Dinge ab (✓), die sie in ihrer Nachbarschaft mag.

1 her neighbours ✓ 2 the sports centre ✓ 3 the big fields ✓ 4 the cars ☐

b) **Complete the sentences with the blue words in Lily's text.**
Vervollständige die Sätze mit den blauen Wörtern aus Lilys Text.

1 Our neighbours are *friendly* . 2 I like the *big* fields.

3 Some places are *dirty* . 4 The cars are very *loud* .

2.16

My neighbourhood

I live on the Whitehawk Estate with my mum and my dad.
My sister doesn't live with us because she's married.
I like our neighbours. They're really friendly. 😊
I like the sports centre because it has interesting activities. 😊
I like the big fields near the estate too. 😊 I walk there with my dad.
But we don't often walk there because he doesn't have a lot of free days.
Some places on the estate are dirty. People don't put rubbish in the bins[1].
And I don't like the cars. They're very loud.
I really like my neighbourhood. I think it's nice!

---

[1] **bin** *Mülltonne*

3 About Lily

Match the two parts of the sentences. Draw lines.
Ordne die beiden Satzteile zu. Ziehe Linien.

1 I don't like	they're very loud.
2 Lily's sister doesn't live at home because	the cars.
3 Lily doesn't like the cars because	she's married.

4 Looking at language **Simple present: negative sentences**

Look again at the sentences in 3. Complete the rule with *don't* or *doesn't*.
Schau dir noch einmal die Sätze in 3 an. Ergänze die Regel mit don't *oder* doesn't.

Wenn wir im *simple present* ausdrücken wollen, dass wir etwas nicht machen, verwenden wir:

I
You
We   *don't*_____ + verb
They

He
She   *doesn't*_____ + verb
It

Scout **likes** rubbish. Lily **doesn't like** rubbish.

5 Your neighbourhood

a) **Do you like these things in your neighbourhood? Draw ☺ or ☹. Write "?" if you don't know.** *Magst du diese Dinge in deiner Nachbarschaft? Male ein ☺ or ☹. Schreibe ein "?", wenn du unsicher bist.*

1 the neighbours _(☺)_   2 the shops _(☹)_   3 the sports centre _(☺)_

4 the school _(☺)_   5 the town centre _(☺)_   6 the youth centre _(?)_

7 *(the beach ☺)*_____   8 *(the park ☹)*_____

b) **Write two more things in the list and add a ☺ or a ☹.**
Ergänze zwei Dinge in der Liste und male ein ☺ oder ein ☹.   ▶ Extra practice 2, p. 133

6 The youth centre

a) **Lily tells her friends about the youth centre. Circle the right verbs.**

Lily erzählt ihren Freunden vom Jugendzentrum. Umkreise die richtigen Verben.

> I go to the youth centre every day. There are a lot of activities like cooking, boxing and football. There's a girls' class on Tuesday, but I (1) **don't go** / doesn't go. Sometimes I play pool at the youth centre with my neighbour Niles. He (2) don't go / **doesn't go** to Varndean and his school (3) don't have / **doesn't have** a lot of clubs. We (4) **don't pay** / doesn't pay for the activities – they're all free.

b) **What about you? Talk to a partner.**

Und du? Sprich mit einem Partner oder einer Partnerin.

I go / I don't go to a youth centre.

I like / I don't   cooking / boxing /
like   football / pool.

> I like cooking. What about you?

> I don't like cooking. I like football. What about you?

▶ Extra practice 3, p. 134

7 Words **Places (1)**

a) **Draw lines from the places to the explanations.**

Ziehe Linien von den Orten zu den Erklärungen.

1 shop	a You can swim here.
2 sports centre	b You watch films here.
3 beach	c You go walking here.
4 cinema	d You do sports here.
5 field	e You buy things here.

b) **Make a mind map for places with the words from a) and more from pages 110–114.**

Erstelle eine Mindmap mit den Wörtern aus a) und weiteren Wörtern von den Seiten 110–114.

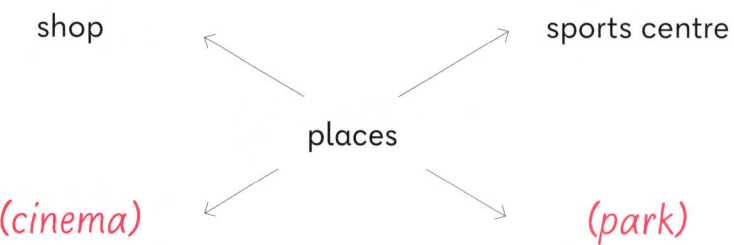

shop   sports centre

places

(cinema)   (park)

▶ Extra practice 4, p. 135

8 Places game

a) *Erstelle eine Tabelle mit neun Orten aus deiner Mindmap von S.114.*

b) *Wenn dein Lehrer oder deine Lehrerin einen Ort beschreibt: melde dich und sage den richtigen Ort. Streiche ihn durch. Wenn du drei Wörter →↓↙↘ hast, rufe "Here!".*

shop	*...*	*...*
...	*...*	*...*
...	*beach*	*...*

9 Reading **My neighbourhood**

Read the posts. (Circle) the right words. *Lies die Posts. Umkreise die richtigen Wörter.*

1 Jing likes / (doesn't like) her neighbourhood.
2 Alexis (likes) / doesn't like his neighbourhood.

I live in a big city. It's very loud. There are a lot of cars.
I don't like my neighbourhood.

Jing, China

I live in a village. There is one shop. My neighbours are friendly.
Sometimes it's boring. I like the fields and animals.

Alexis, France

My task

10 A post about my neighbourhood

Write a post like in 9. Write at least three sentences.
Schreibe einen Post wie in 9. Schreibe mindestens drei Sätze.

I live in a village / a town / a city / the country.
It's cool / boring / busy / loud / nice.
I like ... / I don't like ...

▶ **Digital help**

Ich kann meinen Wohnort beschreiben.

My town or village

1 Places (2)

a) **Match the words and pictures. Write 1–8.**
Ordne die Wörter den Bildern zu. Schreibe 1–8.

1 hospital   2 ice rink   3 library   4 supermarket

5 museum   6 shopping centre   7 stadium   8 train station

b) **Listen and repeat the places in a).** *Höre zu und wiederhole die Orte in a).*
2.17

c) Game *Schreibe die Wörter aus a) auf Kärtchen. Setzt euch in einem Kreis zusammen. Ein Kind nimmt ein Kärtchen und spielt eine zu diesem Ort passende Aktivität vor. Die anderen raten. Wechselt euch ab.*

2 Song **Kasia's town**
2.18

a) **Close your eyes and listen to the song. Does Kasia like her town?**
Schließe deine Augen und höre dir das Lied an. Mag Kasia ihre Stadt?

b) **Listen again. Tick (✓) the places that Kasia's town does not have.**
Höre noch einmal zu. Mache ein Häkchen (✓) an die Dinge, die es in Kasia Stadt nicht gibt.

3 Speaking **Different places**

Partner B: Go to page 132. *Gehe auf die Seite 132.*
Partner A: *Frage, was es in der Stadt deines Partners oder deiner Partnerin gibt.*
Setze ein Häkchen, wenn es diesen Ort gibt. Dann schau dir dein Bild an und
beantworte die Fragen deiner Partnerin oder deines Partners. ▶ Wordbank 11, p. 177

A hospital ☑

An ice rink ☑

A library ☑

A supermarket ☑

A museum ☐

A shopping centre ☑

A stadium ☑

A train station ☐

> Does your town have a museum?

> No, it doesn't.

> Does your town have a hospital?

> Yes, it does.

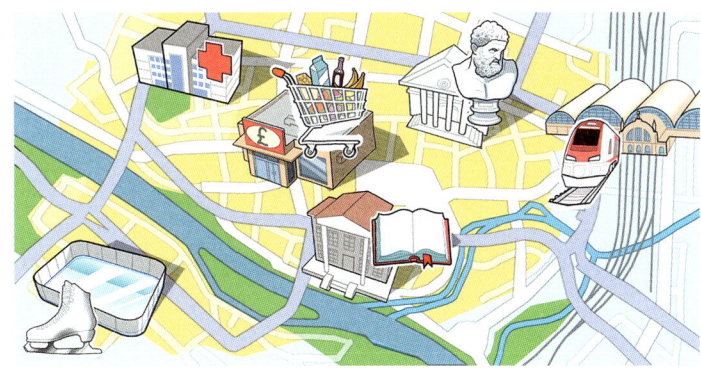

---

4 Looking at language **Simple present: questions and short answers**

Schau dir die Fragen und Antworten an und ergänze die Regel.

1 Do you like your town? – Yes, I do. / No, I don't.
2 Does it have a museum? – Yes, it does. / No, it doesn't.

Wenn du eine Entscheidungsfrage stellst, auf die man mit Ja oder Nein antwortet,
verwendest du am Anfang der Frage das Wort ___*Do*___ (mit *I, you, we, they*) oder
___*Does*___ (mit *he, she, it*).

---

5 **In town with Kasia and Bella**

Match the questions and short answers.
Ordne die Fragen und Kurzantworten einander zu.

Kasia and Bella

1 Does Bella go with you to school?	No, I don't.
2 Do you have problems with Bella in shops?	Yes, she does.
3 Do you and Bella use the bus?	Yes, we do.

6 Towns and visitors

a) (Circle) the right word. *Umkreise das richtige Wort.*

1 (Do)/ Does you have a favourite place in another country?

2 Do /(Does) your town or village have a lot of visitors?

3 (Do)/ Does you visit other places in Germany?

4 Do /(Does) your town have a visitor information centre?

b) **Listen and check.** *Höre zu und prüfe.*
2.19

c) **Talk to a partner. Ask and answer the questions. Give short answers.**
Stellt euch zu zweit die Fragen und beantwortet sie. Gebt Kurzantworten.

Yes, I do. / No, I don't.   *Yes, it does. / No, it doesn't.*

7 Questions from visitors

a) **Listening Listen to four short conversations. Match them with the right pictures.**
2.20
Write 1–4 in the boxes on the pictures. *Höre vier kurze Gespräche.*
Ordne sie den richtigen Bildern zu. Schreibe 1–4 in die Kästchen auf den Bildern.

b) **Listen again. Complete the questions with one word.** *Höre noch einmal zu.*
2.20
Ergänze die Fragen mit einem Wort.

	Yes	No
1 Does bus 12A go to the _beach_ ?	✓	
2 Do you know a good fish and chip _shop_ ?	✓	
3 Does the Brighton Museum open on _Monday_ ?		✓
4 Do you have the _time_ ?	✓	

c) **Does Lily answer yes or no? Tick (✓) the right column – yes or no.** *Antwortet Lily mit Ja oder Nein? Setze in der richtigen Spalte ein Häkchen (✓) – Ja oder Nein.*

d) **Role-play Ask the questions in b) and give short answers.**
Stellt die Fragen in b) und gebt Kurzantworten.

8 Mediation **Welcome to the pier!**

Schau dir die Webseite vom Brighton Pier an und beantworte die Fragen dazu.

1 Wann hat die Seebrücke auf? *von 10 bis 18 Uhr*

2 Muss man dafür Eintritt zahlen? *Nein, es ist umsonst.*

3 Was kann man da tun? *Trampolinspringen, Konzerte, Feuerwerke*

4 Was ist das rosa Zeug auf dem Bild? *eine Art Süßigkeit*

5 Was kann man dort essen? *Fisch und Pommes, Eiskrem*

www.brightonpier.example.com

Brighton Pier is open from 10 am to 6 pm every day. It's free!
There are trampolines, concerts and fireworks.
Buy Brighton Rock – it's pink and sweet.
Eat some fish and chips or an ice cream.

My task

9 Five questions about places

a) *Arbeitet in Gruppen. Entscheidet euch für einen Ort aus der Wordbank auf* S. 177.

b) *Team 1 darf fünf* Yes- *oder* No-*Fragen stellen und versucht den Ort zu erraten.*
Team 2 gibt Kurzantworten. ▶ **Digital help**

c) *Wechselt euch ab.*

Does this place	sell[1]	clothes / drinks[2] / food[3] / …?
	have	books / films / football games / games / old things / table tennis / trains / trees / water[4] / …?
Is it the		beach / cinema / library / museum / park / shopping centre / sports centre / stadium / swimming pool / train station / youth centre / …?

---

[1] **sell** *verkaufen*   [2] **drinks** *Getränke*   [3] **food** *Essen*   [4] **water** *Wasser*

al quiz **Ich kann** über meine Stadt sprechen. ✓

Brighton in all weathers

1 Listening **A walking tour**

a) Before you listen **Look at the pictures. Match them to the correct sentences. Write A–E.**

Schau dir die Bilder an. Ordne sie den passenden Sätzen zu. Schreibe A–E.

1 It's rainy. _D_   2 It's sunny. _A_   3 It's snowy. _E_   4 It's cloudy. _B_   5 It's windy. _C_

A ⟶ 3   B ⟶ 5   C ⟶ 4   D ⟶ 2   E ⟶ 1

2.21

b) **Listen to the walking tour. Put the weather pictures in the right order. Write 1–5 in the boxes at the bottom.**

Höre den Menschen auf dem Rundgang zu. Bringe die Wetterbilder in die richtige Reihenfolge. Schreibe 1–5 unten in die Kästchen.
▶ **Extra practice 5, p. 135**

Erklär-
film

2 Looking at language **Simple present: *wh*-questions**

a) **Read the questions for Eli from people on the tour. Draw lines to Eli's answers.**

Lies die Fragen an Eli von den Teilnehmer/innen des Rundgangs. Ziehe Linien zu Elis Antworten.

1 When does the tower[1] open?	A ticket costs about £10.
2 Why do you love Brighton?	Because it's never boring!
3 Where are you from?	It opens at 10 am.
4 How much does a ticket cost[2]?	It's pink and you can eat it.
5 What is Brighton Rock[3]?	I'm from London.

b) **Write the question words in German.** *Schreibe die Fragewörter auf Deutsch.*

~~wann?~~ • warum? • was? • wie viel? • wo?

1 when? – *wann?*   2 where? – *wo?*   3 when? – *was?*

4 why? – *warum?*   5 how much? – *wie viel?*

[1] **tower** *Turm*   [2] **(to) cost** *kosten*   [3] **Brighton Rock** *Zuckerstange*

3 More questions on the tour

Some people on the tour have questions about Brighton. Put the words in the right order. *Ein paar Menschen auf dem Rundgang haben Fragen zu Brighton. Bringe die Wörter in die richtige Reihenfolge.*

1 the shops / when do / open? <u>When do the shops open</u> ?

2 you / why do / love Brighton? <u>Why do you love Brighton</u> ?

3 does / how much / a bus ticket / cost? <u>How much does a bus ticket cost</u> ?

4 The Upside Down House

Partner B: Look at page 132. *Schau auf Seite 132.*

a) **Partner A: Read the information about the Upside Down House and answer Partner B's questions.**
Partner A: Lies die Informationen zum Upside Down House und beantworte die Fragen von Partner B.

b) **Ask Partner B these questions.**
Stelle Partner B folgende Fragen.

1 When does the Upside Down House open?
2 Where can I buy tickets?
3 How can we take funny photos?

The Upside Down House
You can take cool photos there.
It closes at 9 pm.
Tickets cost £5.

My task

5 Quiz-quiz-swap

a) *Wähle eine Frage aus und schreibe sie auf ein Kärtchen.*

- What do you do when it's hot?
- What do you do when it's rainy?

- Where do you go when it's snowy?
- Where do you go when it's sunny?

b) *Finde eine Partnerin oder einen Partner und stelle deine Frage. Beantworte die Frage deiner Partnerin oder deines Partners.*

When it's hot,
I go swimming.

c) *Tauscht die Karten, geht weiter und stellt eure neue Frage einem neuen Kind.*

▶ **Digital help**

▶ Extra practice 6, p. 136

Lily's idea

1 Before you read **Where Lily lives**

What can you remember about Lily's neighbourhood? Collect ideas with your class. *Was weißt du noch über Lilys Nachbarschaft? Sammle Ideen in deiner Klasse.*

> She lives on an estate.

> The neighbours are friendly.

2 Reading **Clean-up day**

a) **Lily makes a poster for a clean-up day on her estate. Read the first sentence of the story and complete the poster.**
Lily macht ein Poster für einen Aufräumtag in ihrer Siedlung. Lies den ersten Satz der Story und ergänze das Poster.

HELLO, NEIGHBOURS!

Come to our clean-up day

When? 9am, *Sunday* 2 April

Where? At the *youth centre*

b) **Read the story. What does Buddy find?** *Lies die Geschichte. Was findet Buddy?*

2.22

It's 9 am on Sunday morning and there's a
big group in front of the youth centre.
'It's a great idea to have a clean-up day, Lily!'
says her sister Chloe.
5 'And it's great you have new friends!'
'Yes, it is. Noah, Sunita, Zane – this is my
sister Chloe,' says Lily.
'Hi guys[1]! Nice to meet you. And who is this?'
'It's my dog, Buddy,' says Noah.
10 'Hello, everybody. Welcome to clean-up day!'
says Lily's mum. 'We have a lot of big rubbish
bags. And we can put good things for the
Swap Place over there.'

---

[1] **guys** *Leute*

2.23

Lily, Chloe and Noah work together.
15 Buddy wants to help too. First he finds a dead mouse. Next Buddy brings an old shoe to Lily. 'Thanks, Buddy,' says Lily. Then Buddy digs in the ground for a long time. 'What do you have now?'
20 asks Noah. 'It's a gold ring. 'It has "Jack and Maria" in it.'
'The ring looks old,' says Chloe.
'But how do we find Jack and Maria?'
The neighbours meet at the youth
25 centre at 12 o'clock. They have over fifty bags of rubbish! And some chairs, a

bike, shoes and other things for the Swap Place in the youth centre.
They eat lunch and Lily tells the others
30 about the ring.
'Why don't you put a note in the youth centre?' asks Zane. 'Maybe[1] somebody knows Jack and Maria.'
Two days later a boy phones Lily's mum.
35 'My name's Davy,' he says. 'Maria is my grandma. She is really happy about her ring! My grandparents want to give the youth centre some money to say thank you.'

3 People in the story

Complete the sentences. *Vervollständige die Sätze.*

1 Chloe is Lily's *sister*.

2 Buddy is Noah's *dog*.

3 Jack and *Maria* are the names on the ring.

4 Maria is Davy's *grandma*.

4 Why, what and how?

Answer the questions. *Beantworte die Fragen.*

1 What three things does Buddy find? A *mouse*, a *shoe* and a *ring*.

2 How many bags of rubbish does the group collect? Over *fifty*.

3 Why does Davy's grandma give the youth centre money? To say *thank you*.

[1] **maybe** *vielleicht*

5   Words in the text

Find the words in the text and write them next to the correct German word.
Finde die Wörter im Text und schreibe sie neben die passenden deutschen Wörter.

1   Müll *(line 12)*   *rubbish*

2   Tausch *(line 13)*   *swap*

3   buddeln *(line 19)*   *dig*

4   Erde *(line 19)*   *ground*

5   Zettel *(line 33)*   *note*

6   Geld *(line 41)*   *money*

6   The Whitehawk Swap Place

True (✓) or false (✗)? *Richtig (✓) oder falsch (✗)?*

1   Things for the Swap Place are things that other people can use.   ✓

2   The neighbours don't find a lot of things for the Swap Place.   ✗

3   The Swap Place is in the youth centre.   ✓

7   Life skills **Go Green!**

a)   *Organisiert eine Tauschbörse bei euch in der Klasse oder in der Schule. Was könnt ihr tauschen? Erstellt dazu eine Mindmap.*

b)   *Macht ein Info-Poster für die Tauschbörse.*

Hi students

Do you want to swap some of your things with other students?

For example, books, ... Why don't you ...?
...

I use a lot of things from other people.

c)   *Wählt das beste Poster. Dann fangt an, eure Sachen zu tauschen!*

---

[1] **toys** *Spielzeug*

Digital quiz    **Ich kann** **eine Geschichte lesen und verstehen.**

The Brighton dares: In town

1 In Brighton

Before you watch *Schau dir die Fotos an und lies den Text. Entscheide für jede Wette, ob es eine schwere oder eine leichte ist.*

Emir

Change[1] the time on the Queen's Park Clock Tower[2].

Daisy

Give a free[3] tour of Brighton to a tourist (in a swimming cap[4]).

> *I think Daisy's dare[5] is …*

> *I think Emir's dare is …*

2 Viewing **The dares**

Schau dir das Video an. Ordne die Sätze 1–4 den Personen A–D zu.

1 Does the tour go down to the beach?
2 It's always correct.

3 You can always do the dares!
4 Sorry, Daisy. I have to go now.

A **2** Clock master

B **3** Gloria

C **1** Mara

D **4** Joe

3 Try Emir's trick

a) *Schreibe den Namen von einem Ort in Brighton auf. Schau in den Spiegel und schreibe das Wort nach. Oder schau auf die gespiegelten Buchstaben in der Tabelle.*

b) *Lies das Wort von deinem Partner oder deiner Partnerin. Benutze einen Spiegel oder die Tabelle.*

```
ABCDEFGHIJKLM
NOPQRSTUVWXYZ
WOԀOꓤƧ⊥ՈɅMX⅄Ƨ
ABCDEFGHIJKLM
```

---

[1] **change** *verändern*   [2] **tower** *Turm*   [3] **free** *umsonst*   [4] **swimming cap** *Badekappe*
[5] **dare** *Mutprobe*

Give a presentation

1 Collect ideas

Help Scout to give a presentation about her favourite place: the beach. Collect words and ideas about the beach. Look at pages 12–13 for more ideas.

Hilf Scout eine Präsentation über ihren Lieblingsplatz zu halten: den Strand. Sammle Wörter und Ideen zum Thema Strand. Auf den Seiten 12–13 findest du weitere Anregungen.

Help me plan a presentation, please.

(lots of people, fish and chips, picnic, play football, swim, seagulls, picnic, sandwiches)

2 Make slides

My favourite place
- favourite place
- Brighton beach
- a lot of people
- fish and chips

1 Finde ein schönes, großes Foto.
2 Mach den Titel groß.
3 Schreibe kurze Notizen zum Foto.
4 Gestalte es schön und bunt.

3 Make a structure

2.24

a) **Now listen to Scout's talk. Put the parts in the right order. Write 1–4.** *Nun höre dir Scouts Präsentation an. Bringe die Teile in die richtige Reihenfolge. Schreibe 1–4.*

3 I like it because there are a lot of people. They often eat fish and chips.

4 Thank you for listening. Do you have questions?

1 Hello. This presentation is about my favourite place.

2 My favourite place is Brighton beach.

b) **Give Scout's presentation to your partner. Then swap roles.** *Trage Scouts Präsentation deinem Partner oder deiner Partnerin vor. Dann tauscht die Rollen.*

Digital quiz 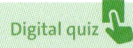   **Ich kann** eine kurze Präsentation vorbereiten. ✓

Present your top three places for kids

Step 1

Arbeitet in Gruppen mit einer Placemat. Malt eine Placemat auf ein großes Stück Papier. Jede Gruppe überlegt sich zunächst drei Orte in der Nachbarschaft, die für Kinder geeignet sind und jedes Kind schreibt seine Ideen in einen Teil der Placemat. Dann entscheidet euch zusammen für die besten drei Orte und schreibt sie in die Mitte der Placemat.

the cinema
the shopping centre
the park

the skatepark
the cinema
the park

the park
the cinema
the science museum

the park
the science museum
the youth centre

the park
the city centre
the science museum

▶ Wordbank 11, p. 177

Step 2

Findet für jeden Ort ein Foto und macht euch ein paar Notizen dazu, z.B.:

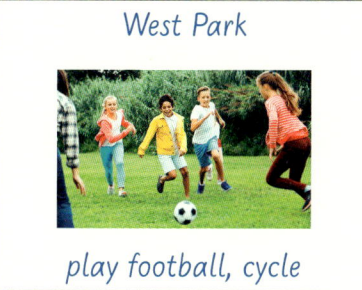
West Park

play football, cycle

Bali Kino

good on rainy days

Kindermuseum

great, free

▶ Digital help

Step 3

Schaut euch eure Notizen aus Step 2 an und bereitet eure Präsentation vor.

Hello. This presentation is about our top three places for kids.
My favourite place for kids is ...
I like it because ...
Thank you for listening. Do you have questions?

Step 4

Haltet eure Präsentation. Nutzt euren Text aus Step 3.
Versucht frei zu sprechen und den Text nicht einfach nur abzulesen.

1 Mediation **Jack's favourite place**

Ich kann Informationen über Brighton verstehen.

Read the message from your British friend Jack. Answer the questions in German. *Lies die Nachricht von deinem britischen Freund Jack. Beantworte die Fragen auf Deutsch.*

> Hi!
> Hove Skatepark is my favourite place. I often go skateboarding there.
> It's not in the town centre, but there's a train station and a bus stop next to the park.
> It's free and it's always open!
> Jack

1 Was ist Jacks Lieblingsort?

Hove Skatepark

2 Wie kommt man dorthin?

Man kann mit dem Bus oder mit der Bahn hinfahren.

3 Muss man Eintritt zahlen?

Nein, es ist kostenlos.

4 Bis wann ist der Skatepark offen?

Er ist immer offen.

2 Language **We live in Hove**

Ich kann meine Nachbarschaft beschreiben.

Read Sunita's sentences and complete them with *don't* or *doesn't*.
Lies Sunitas Sätze und ergänze sie mit don't *oder* doesn't.

1 Hove has nice shops and parks, but it *doesn't* have a cinema.

2 There's a museum, but I *don't* go there very often.

3 I *don't* like museums!

4 I like Hove, but Ben *doesn't* like it.

5 He wants to live in London, but my mum *doesn't* want to live there!

Check

3 A tour of Chester

a) Language Zane visits his cousin Sophie and asks questions about her town. Fill in the gaps with *do / does / doesn't*.

Zane besucht seine Cousine Sophie und stellt ihr Fragen zu ihrer Stadt. Ergänze die Lücken mit do / does / doesn't.

Zane   _Do_ you like your town?

Sophie   Yes, I _do_ .

Zane   _Does_ your town have a good park?

Sophie   Yes, it _does_ .

Zane   _Does_ your town have a beach?

Sophie   No, it _doesn't_ .

b) Words Write the letters a–f next to the right words.

Schreibe die Buchstaben a–f neben die richtigen Wörter.

a  b 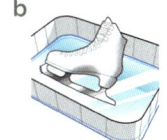 c  d 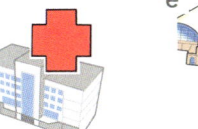 e  f

1 train station _e_   2 supermarket _c_   3 library _f_

4 stadium _a_   5 ice rink _b_   6 hospital _d_

c) Listening Listen to the tour. Where do Zane and Sophie go? Put the pictures in the right order. Write 1–6.

Höre dem Rundgang zu. Wohin gehen Zane und Sunita? Bringe die Bilder in die richtige Reihenfolge.

2  6  1

5 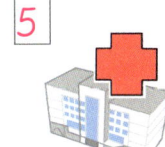 3  4

Check

VARNDEAN
Teen Zine

Our school magazine

Questions and answers: The Real Junk Food Project

What is it ?
It's a cafe in Brighton. It uses waste[1] food
and there are no prices[2].

Where does the food come from?
When shops in Brighton don't sell[3] all their
food, they don't put the rest in the bin – they
give it to the cafe!

How much do meals cost?
You pay what you can.
And everybody sits together!

Puzzle time

Where in Brighton am I?

1   I'm not land and I'm not sea
    But to walk on water
    You can walk on me!

2   I'm high in the sky
    With a big round[4] eye
    But I'm not a bird and I can't fly!

---

[1] **waste** *überschüssig; hier: Lebensmittel, die weggeworfen werden sollten*   [2] **price** *Preis*
[3] **sell** *verkaufen*   [4] **round** *rund*

A postcard from Brighton

Dear Annie
Brighton is great!
My favourite place here is Snooper's Paradise.
It's a really cool shop and it sells
everything[5]! Hats, skateboards, photos,
guitars, clocks, toys, books, posters ...
It's very big.
What's your favourite shop?

Leena xx

Fergal's reading tip

My favourite book is 'A Brighton birthday'.
It's a cool story with lots of places in
Brighton and I love the puzzles too!

It's Saturday morning and Alice wakes up. It's her birthday! But there are no birthday messages, no presents and everybody is busy. What's happening? Then she gets a mysterious[6] message with a puzzle ...

---

[5] **everything** *alles*   [6] **mysterious** *geheimnisvoll*

👥 **3** Speaking **Different places**   ▶ page 117

Partner B: Schau dir das Bild von deiner Stadt an und beantworte die Fragen deines Partners oder deiner Partnerin. Dann frage, was es in deren Stadt gibt. Setze ein Häkchen (✓) hinter den Ort, wenn es ihn gibt.

> Does your town have a hospital?

> Yes, it does.

> Does your town have a stadium?

> No, it doesn't.

1 A hospital ✓   2 An ice rink ✓   3 A library ✓   4 A supermarket ✓

5 A museum ✓   6 A shopping centre ☐   7 A stadium ☐   8 A train station ✓

👥 **4** **The Upside Down House**   ▶ page 121

a) **Ask Partner A these questions.**
Stelle Partner A diese Fragen.

   1 What can you do in the Upside Down House?
   2 When does it close?
   3 How much do tickets cost?

b) **Read the information and answer Partner A's questions.**
Lies die Informationen und beantworte die Fragen von Partner A.

The Upside Down House
It opens at 10 am.
You can buy tickets at the kiosk.
You can take funny photos:
put your hands up and then turn[1] the photo.

---

¹ **turn sth. over** *etwas drehen*

▶ page 111

Extra practice 1

a) **What about your town? Write the names of these places in *your* town.**
Was ist mit deiner Stadt? Schreibe die Namen dieser Orte in deiner Stadt auf.

1 There are cool shops here. _____

2 This is a good place for a picnic. _____

3 You can watch films here. _____

4 You can go skateboarding here. _____

5 You can eat pizza here. _____

b) **Compare with a partner. Did you write the same places?** *Vergleiche mit einem Partner oder einer Partnerin. Habt ihr dieselben Orte aufgeschrieben?*

▶ page 113

Extra practice 2

a) *Male etwas zu essen, das dir nicht schmeckt.*

b) *Arbeitet in kleinen Gruppen: Zeigt einander eure Bilder. Sagt abwechselnd, was auf den Bildern zu sehen ist.*

> *You don't like fish.*

c) *Erzählt der Klasse von den anderen in eurer Gruppe.*

> *Jashan doesn't like fish. Mariam doesn't like pizza.*

► page 1

Extra practice 3

a) **Complete the sentences about Amelie with *likes / doesn't like*.**
Vervollständige die Sätze über Amelie mit likes / doesn't like.

AMELIE

singing ☹	1	Amelie *doesn't like* singing.
dancing ☺	2	She *likes* dancing.
cricket ☹	3	She *doesn't like* cricket.
trampolining ☺	4	She *likes* trampolining.
playing computer games ☹	5	She *doesn't like* playing computer games.
cycling ☺	6	She *likes* cycling.
listening to music ☺	7	She *likes* listening to music.
swimming ☹	8	She *doesn't like* swimming.

b) **What about you? Draw ☺ or ☹. Write sentences about you with *like / don't like*.**
Und du? Male ☺ *oder* ☹. *Schreibe Sätze über dich mit* like / don't like.

ME

singing	1	I *(don't like)* singing.
dancing	2	I *(like)* dancing.
cricket	3	I *(like)* cricket.
trampolining	4	I *(don't like)* trampolining.
playing computer games	5	I *(don't like)* playing computer games.
cycling	6	I *(like)* cycling.
listening to music	7	I *(like)* listening to music.
swimming	8	I *(don't like)* swimming.

Extra practice 4 ▶ page 114

Complete the sentences with the words from the box.

Vervollständige die Sätze mit Wörtern aus der Box.

cafe • cinema • ~~shop~~ • skatepark • sports centre

1 You buy things in a *shop* .

2 You drink[1] hot chocolate in a *cafe* .

3 You can play football and basketball at the *sports centre* .

4 You can go skateboarding at the *skatepark* .

5 You can watch films at the *cinema* .

Extra practice 5 ▶ page 120

a) **Write the correct weather word in each sentence. Go back to page 120 if you don't know.** *Schreibe in jeden Satz das richtige Wetter-Wort. Schau auf Seite 120 nach, wenn du unsicher bist.*

Monday	Tuesday	Wednesday	Thursday	Friday

1 On Monday it's *sunny* .

2 On Tuesday it's *cloudy* .

3 On Wednesday it's *windy* .

4 On Thursday it's *rainy* .

5 On Friday it's *snowy* .

b) **What's the weather like today in your town?** *Wie ist das Wetter heute in deiner Stadt?*

It's *(cloudy and rainy)* .

---

[1] **drink** *trinken*

Extra practice 6 ▶ page 121

a) Draw lines from the questions to the right answers.

Zeichne Linien von den Fragen zur richtigen Antwort.

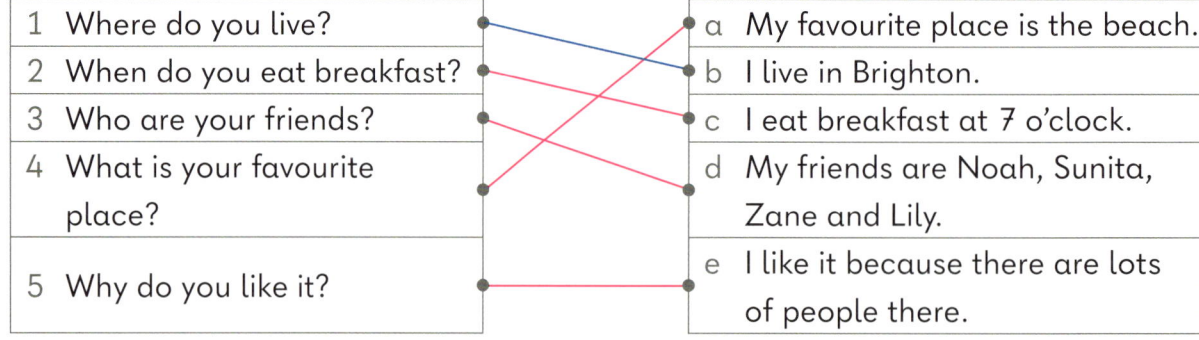

1 Where do you live?	a My favourite place is the beach.
2 When do you eat breakfast?	b I live in Brighton.
3 Who are your friends?	c I eat breakfast at 7 o'clock.
4 What is your favourite place?	d My friends are Noah, Sunita, Zane and Lily.
5 Why do you like it?	e I like it because there are lots of people there.

b) Answer the questions for you. Write sentences.

Beantworte die Fragen für dich. Schreibe ganze Sätze.

1 I live in *(Rostock)* _____ .

2 I wake up at *(6.30)* _____ .

3 My friends are *(Amina, Dilay and Lena)* _____ .

4 My favourite place is *(the swimming pool)* _____ .

5 I like it because *(I like swimming)* _____ .

c) Write the words in English.

Schreibe die Wörter in Englisch auf.

1 wo? – *where?*   2 wann? – *when?*   3 wer? – *who?*

4 was? – *what?*   5 warum? – *why?*

🔊 Unit 4 – Where I live

pp. 110/111 **cinema**   das Kino

pier   der Pier, die Seebrücke

shop   das Geschäft, der Laden

picnic   das Picknick

chips *(pl)*   die Pommes frites   **fish and chips** = Fisch mit Pommes Frites

Topic 1

▶ p. 112 **(to) hear**   hören

field   das Feld; die Weide

neighbourhood   die Nachbarschaft, die Gegend, das Viertel

married (to)   verheiratet (mit)

interesting   interessant

estate   die Wohnsiedlung; das Gewerbegebiet

dirty   schmutzig

(to) put   *(etwas wohin)* tun, legen, stellen, stecken

rubbish   der (Haus-)Müll, der Abfall

▶ p. 113 **town**   die Stadt

youth   die Jugend; der Jugendliche

▶ p. 114 **(to) box**   boxen

(to) pay (for sth.)   (etwas be)zahlen

(to) buy   kaufen

▶ p. 115 **village**   das Dorf

boring   langweilig

country   das Land, *(auch:)* die ländliche Gegend

Topic 2

▶ p. 116 **hospital**   das Krankenhaus

ice rink   die Schlittschuhbahn

library   die Bücherei, die Bibliothek

supermarket   der Supermarkt

museum   das Museum

stadium   das Stadion

(train) station der Bahnhof

▶ p. 118	**another**	ein/e andere/r/s
	visitor	der Besucher, die Besucherin; der Gast
	(to) **visit**	besuchen
	other	andere(r, s)
	Germany	Deutschland
	information	die Information(en)

Topic 3

▶ p. 120	**rainy**	regnerisch
	sunny	sonnig
	snowy	schneebedeckt; verschneit
	cloudy	wolkig, bewölkt
	windy	windig
	when?	wann?
	much	viel; sehr
	How much?	Wie viel?
▶ p. 121	**upside down**	verkehrt herum, auf dem Kopf
	funny	witzig, lustig; seltsam
	hot	heiß, warm

Story

▶ p. 122	**clean-up**	das Säubern, das Saubermachen
	morning	der Morgen
	in the morning	am Morgen, morgens
	group	die Gruppe
	Welcome to ...	Willkommen in/an/bei ...
	bag	die Tasche, der Beutel
	swap	der Tausch
	(to) **swap**	tauschen
▶ p. 123	**together**	zusammen
	first	zuerst, als Erstes
	(to) **find**	finden
	dead	tot
	mouse, *pl* mice	die Maus two mice
	Next ...	Als Nächstes ...
	(to) **bring**	bringen, mitbringen
	shoe	der Schuh
	(to) **dig**	buddeln, graben

ring	der Ring
note	die Notiz; der kurze Brief
somebody	jemand
(to) phone	anrufen; telefonieren
grandparents *(pl)*	die Großeltern
many	viele
(to) collect	(ein)sammeln

much („viel") – many („viele")
How much time do we have?   We don't have much time, but we have a lot of work.
Wie viel Zeit ...?   nicht viel Zeit   viel Arbeit
How many shops are in your village?   There aren't many shops, but there are a lot of fields.
Wie viele Geschäfte ...?   nicht viele Geschäfte   viele Felder

▶ p. 124	example	das Beispiel
	for example	zum Beispiel

Unit 5
Enjoy!

My favourite food is trifle. In trifle there is fruit and cream. A lot of people put strawberries on trifle, but I'm allergic to strawberries.

fruit

cream

1 Words **Food**

a) *Lest Noahs und Sunitas Texte zu zweit. Manche Wörter sind ähnlich wie im Deutschen. Wie lauten sie auf Deutsch? Schlagt die unbekannten Wörter in eurem Vocabulary auf Seite 166 nach.*

1 fruit	*Frucht*	2 cream	*Sahne*	3 tomato	*Tomate*
4 sauce	*Soße*	5 bread	*Brot*	6 rice	*Reis*

b) **Listen and repeat all the words in blue in Noah's and Sunita's texts.**
2.26   *Höre zu und wiederhole alle Wörter in Blau in Noahs und Sunitas Texten.*

Nach dieser Unit kann ich ...

○ über Essen sprechen
○ über Geburtstage und Feste sprechen
○ mein Lieblingsgericht beschreiben
○ über Unterschiede sprechen
○ unbekannte Wörter erklären

Unit task

○ ein Rezeptbuch erstellen

> *I don't eat meat. My favourite food is mattar paneer. It's Indian cheese and peas in a tomato sauce. We eat it with bread or rice and some vegetables.*

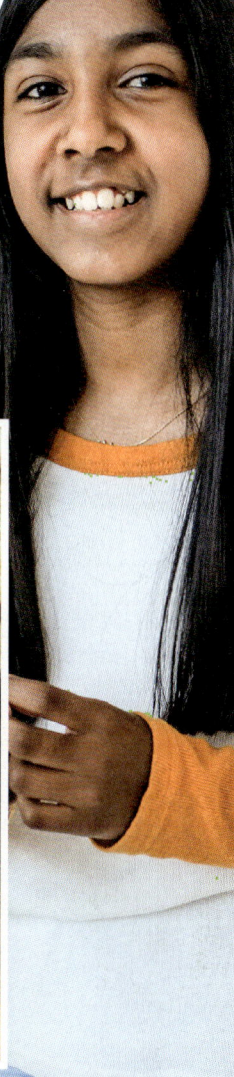

2 Speaking Our food

a) **Read the texts again. Complete the sentences.**
   Lies die Texte noch einmal. Ergänze die Sätze.

   1 In trifle there is *fruit* and *cream* .

   2 Noah is allergic to *strawberries* .

   3 Mattar paneer is *(Indian) cheese* and *peas* in a *tomato sauce* .

b) **What about you? Talk about the food on these pages.**
   Und du? Sprich über das Essen auf diesen Seiten.

   I like ...   I don't like ...

Time for a party

1 Reading **Noah's invitation**

a) Before you read **What do you do on your birthday? Tell a partner.**
Was machst du an deinem Geburtstag? Tauscht euch zu zweit aus.

> I sometimes have a party.

> I always eat cake.

> I go to the cinema.

b) **Read Noah's invitation. Answer the questions.**
Lies Noahs Einladung. Beantworte die Fragen.

1 **What day** is the party?

Saturday

2 **What time** does the party start?

2 o'clock

3 **Where** is the party?

at the skatepark

4 **What food** can you eat at the party?

picnic food

COME TO
Noah's 12
BIRTHDAY PARTY!
- Saturday, 30th May
- 2 o'clock
- At the skatepark
- Play circus party games and eat picnic food

▶ Extra practice 1, p. 161

2 Words **Months**

2.27

a) Song **Listen and sing. Then listen again and stand up when you hear your birthday month.** *Höre zu und singe. Höre dann noch einmal zu und stehe auf, wenn du deinen Geburtstagsmonat hörst.*

January	February	March	April
May	June	July	August
September	October	November	December

b) Walk around **Talk to five people. Ask when their birthday month is.**
Sprich mit fünf anderen Kindern. Frage nach ihrem Geburtstagsmonat.

> When's your birthday?

> It's in March. When's your birthday?

> It's in December.

▶ Extra practice 2, p. 161

3 Birthday dates

🔊 2.29
a) **Look at the list of numbers on page 168. Listen and repeat.** *Sieh dir die* List of numbers *auf Seite 168 an. Höre zu und wiederhole.*

My birthday is on the first of April.

🔊 2.30
b) **Listen to six students. Write their birthdays.** *Höre sechs Kindern zu. Schreibe ihre Geburtstage auf.*

1 **Noah:** *30* th May

2 **Lily:** *15* th April

3 **Zane:** *3* rd August

4 **Sunita:** *2* nd March

5 **Theo:** *11* th February

6 **Ivy:** *19* th January

👥 4 Speaking **My birthday**

a) *Macht zwei Gruppen. Stellt euch in jeder Gruppe in der Reihenfolge eurer Geburtstage hintereinander auf. Welche Gruppe war schneller?*

b) *Überprüft: Stehen alle an der richtigen Stelle? Nennt eure Geburtstage.*

When's your birthday?

It's on the twenty-first of May. What about you?

5 Writing **My birthday invitation**

a) *Sieh dir Noahs Einladung auf Seite 142 noch einmal an. Schreibe eine Einladung zu deinem Geburtstag. Die Einladung sollte echt aussehen!*

b) **Gallery walk** **Look at all the invitations. Which one do you like best?** *Sieh dir alle Einladungen an. Welche gefällt dir am besten?*

I like this invitation[1] best.

This is my favourite invitation.

▶ Extra practice 3, p. 162

---

[1] invitation *Einladung*

6 Zane calls Noah

Sieh dir das Bild rechts an und lies das Telefongespräch zwischen Zane und Noah. Siehst du den Unterschied? Was machen Noah und Buddy wirklich?

1 Noah is playing with Buddy / (juggling).

2 Buddy is playing ball / (watching Noah).

Zane _____ Hi, Noah! What are you doing?

Noah _____ Hi, Zane. I'm not telling you. It's a secret …
I'm playing with Buddy. Yes, … he's playing
ball now.

Erklär-
film

7 Looking at language **Present progressive**

Vervollständige die Sätze aus dem Dialog in 6.

What are you _doing_ ?

I'm not _telling_ you.

I'm _playing_ with Buddy.

He's _playing_ ball now.

> Mit dem *present progressive* sprechen wir darüber, was in diesem Moment (*now, at the moment*) geschieht.
> Wir bilden das *present progressive* mit **am / is / are** und dem Verb + **ing**:
> **I'm** play**ing** with Buddy.

8 Double circle **What are you doing?**

Have a phone call with different partners. Use the ideas in the box.
Mache mehrere Telefonanrufe. Nutze die Ideen in der Box.

> eating a kebab • playing with my pet snake • coding •
> playing on my phone • watching a film • looking at a comic

Hi! What are you doing?

I'm eating a kebab. What are you doing?

I'm watching a film. OK – see you!

9 A birthday photo

Zane zeigt seiner Mutter ein Foto der Geburtstagsfeier seines Freundes.
Vervollständige die Sätze mit den Wörtern in der Box.

> 's taking • is drawing • ~~'m eating~~ • are dancing • is sitting

1 I'm eating birthday cake.

2 Sunita and Ruby are dancing .

3 Noah is sitting on a chair.

4 He's taking photos with his phone.

5 Lily is drawing a picture.

10 Speaking **Find the differences**

Partner A: Sieh dir das Bild unten an. Partner B: Sieh dir das Bild auf Seite 160 an.
Beschreibt von 1–6, was ihr seht. Wechselt euch ab und findet sechs Unterschiede.

> singing • talking • looking at a comic •
> eating strawberries • sleeping[1] •
> playing with her phone

Number 1: In my picture a boy and a girl are singing.

In my picture they are talking.

▶ Extra practice 4–5, pp. 162–163

My task

11 My party photos

Zeigt einander Fotos von Familienfeiern. Beschreibt sie. Ihr könnt auch die
Fotos auf Seite 160 beschreiben.
This is my birthday party. It's 26th of February. My sister is playing with our cat.
We're eating cake and watching a film.

▶ Digital help

---

[1] **sleep** *schlafen*

Party shopping

1 Listening **A present for Noah**

a) Before you listen **What does Noah like? What doesn't Noah like? Put 😊 or 😞.**

Was mag Noah? Was mag Noah nicht? Zeichne 😊 oder 😞.

animals 😊 _____ circus tricks 😊 _____ strawberries 😞 _____

🔊 2.32 b) *Sunita und Lily suchen online nach einem Geburtstagsgeschenk für Noah. Sieh dir die Webseite an. Höre zu. Umkreise, was sie kaufen.*

🔊 2.32 c) *Höre noch einmal zu. Setze ein Häkchen (✓) neben die Sätze, die du hörst.*

😊 1 It's a great present. ✓   2 That's a good idea. ✓   3 That's perfect. ✓

😞 4 It's boring. ☐   5 It's too expensive¹. ✓   6 I don't like it. ☐

---

2 Speaking **Find a present**

a) *Sammelt Ideen für schöne Geburtstagsgeschenke. Schreibt sie an die Tafel.*

b) *Wählt ein Geschenk für jedes Kind in eurer Gruppe.*   Let's find a present for Samir.

What about a bike?   It's too expensive.   That's perfect.

c) *Das „Geburtstagskind" bedankt sich und sagt etwas zum Geschenk.*

Thank you! It's a cool present!

---

¹ **expensive** *teuer*

3 Listening **Party food and drinks**

 2.33

Sieh dir die Speisekarte für Noahs Party an. Höre Noah und seinen Eltern zu. Ein Wort ist falsch. Streiche es durch.

Noah's party menu[1]

hot dogs
pasta salad
carrots
melon

~~cola~~
lemonade

---

4 Words **The shopping list**

 2.34

a) **Read the conversation. Write Noah's shopping list for his party.**
Lies das Gespräch. Schreibe Noahs Einkaufszettel für seine Party.

Noah	___	How much bread do we need?
Dad	___	Two packets.
Noah	___	OK. And how many sausages?
Dad	___	Twenty sausages.
Noah	___	How much pasta?
Dad	___	One big bag.
Noah	___	And how many carrots? One bag?
Dad	___	Yes. And one big melon.
Noah	___	How many lemons do we need for the lemonade? And how much sugar?
Dad	___	Twelve lemons. We already have sugar.

Shopping list

__2__ packets bread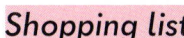
__20__ sausages
__1__ big bag pasta
__1__ bag carrots
__1__ big melon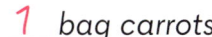
__12__ lemons

 2.35

b) **Listen and check.** *Höre zu und überprüfe deine Antworten.*

---

5 Looking at language **How much? How many?**

 klär-
m

a) *Ergänze die Tabelle mit den Wörtern zum Essen aus 4a).*

How much ...?	How many ...?
bread , *pasta* , *sugar*	*sausages* , *carrots* , *lemons*
Diese Wörter sind *unzählbar* .	Diese Wörter sind *zählbar* .

b) *Schreibe zählbar oder unzählbar unter die Wörter in der Tabelle in 5a).*

---

[1] menu *Speisekarte*

6 Game *How much ...? How many ...? – A lot of ...!*

a) *Sieh dir das Bild an. Schreibe vier Fragen für deinen Partner / deine Partnerin auf.*

1 How many *strawberries* are there?   *Not many.*

2 How many *(tomatoes)* are there?   *(A lot.)*

3 How much *(pasta)* is there?   *(A lot.)*

4 How much *(cheese)* is there?   *(Not much.)*

b) *Stelle deinem Partner / deiner Partnerin deine Fragen von* 6a)*. Einigt euch auf die richtigen Antworten:* Not much. / Not many. / A lot. *Schreibe die Antworten auf. Tauscht die Rollen.*

▶ Extra practice 6, p. 164

> **not much** nicht viel (*unzählbar*) • **not many** nicht viele (*zählbar*) • **a lot** viel / viele

 7 Song **The shopping song**

2.36

a) **Listen to the song. Circle the words you hear.**
Höre dir das Lied an. Umkreise die Wörter, die du hörst.

> I'm going to the shop / (supermarket) today[1].
> Where's my (shopping list) / phone? I'm on my way.
> I have my (bags) / bike and my money 'cause[2] I
> Have a lot of fish / (food) I need to[3] buy.

b) **Listen again and sing.** *Höre noch einmal zu. Singe mit.*

---

[1] **today** heute   [2] **'cause** weil   [3] **need to** müssen

8 Mediation **A party game**

Dein Freund möchte wissen, wie dieses Spiel gespielt wird. Beantworte seine Fragen auf Deutsch: a) Was brauchst du zum Spielen? b) Wie spielst du es?

> *Du brauchst Schokolade, einen Teller, ...* ✓

> *Du würfelst. Wenn du eine 6 bekommst, ...* ✓

The chocolate game

You need:

plate
chocolate
fork
knife

- some chocolate on a plate
- a knife and a fork
- sunglasses ⟶
- gloves ⟶
- a dice ⟶

To play:

- Roll the dice. If you get a six, you can play.
- Put on the sunglasses and gloves. Eat the chocolate with the knife and fork.
- Eat quickly! The next person with a six wants to eat the chocolate too.
- The game finishes when there is no more chocolate.

My task

9 Our party

a) *Plant eine Klassenparty. Arbeitet in Gruppen.*

> dance party • film party • garden party • magic party • ...

> *Let's have a garden party!*
> *What about a film party?*

b) *Macht Notizen zu:* party food, party music, games and activities.

c) *Erzählt der Klasse über eure Party. Die Klasse wählt den besten Partyplan.*

> *We want to have a ... party.*
> *This is our party food: ...*
> *This is our party music: ...*
> *Our games and activities are: ...*

▶ Digital help 🔖 ▶ Wordbank 12, p. 178

Let's cook!

1 Before you watch **A shopping list for a chocolate cake**

Write the words under the correct picture.
Schreibe die Wörter unter das richtige Bild.

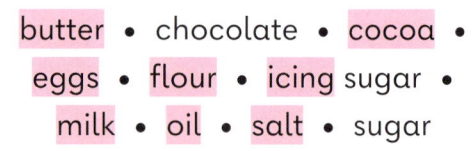

butter • chocolate • cocoa •
eggs • flour • icing sugar •
milk • oil • salt • sugar

1  f*lour*

2 oil

3  s*ugar*

4 c*ocoa*

5 m*ilk*

6  e*ggs*

7  s*alt*

8  b*utter*

9  c*hocolate*

10 i*cing sugar*

2 Viewing **A cooking video**

a) *Schau dir das Video an. Bringe die Fotos in die richtige Reihenfolge. Schreibe 1–6.*

4 — He's putting the mixture in the oven[1].

1 — He's breaking[2] the eggs.

6 — He's putting the icing on the cake.

3 — He's adding the flour and cocoa.

2 — He's mixing the eggs, oil, sugar and salt.

5 — He's making the icing with chocolate, butter and sugar.

b) **Watch again and check.** *Schau das Video noch mal an und überprüfe deine Antwort.*

[1] **oven** *Backofen* [2] **break** *zerbrechen*

3 Reading Zane's favourite dish

🔊
2.37

a) Read Zane's text. *Lies Zanes Text.*

www.cooking-with-zane.example.net

This is my favourite dish. It's jollof rice. It comes from Nigeria.

You make it with rice, tomatoes, onions, peppers and chicken. I love it!

You eat it with plantain¹. Plantain is a kind of banana.

My dad cooks it every week. And sometimes I cook it too.

¹ **plantain** *Kochbanane*

b) Read the text again. Are these sentences true or false? Circle.
Lies den Text noch einmal. Sind diese Sätze richtig oder falsch? Kreise ein.

1	Zane's favourite dish comes from India.	true / (false)
2	Jollof rice has meat in it.	(true) / false
3	Plantain is a kind of banana.	(true) / false
4	Zane's dad cooks jollof rice every day.	true / (false)
5	Zane sometimes cooks it.	(true) / false

My task

4 My favourite dish

Write about your favourite dish. Use Zane's text in 3 and these questions to help you. *Schreibe über dein Lieblingsessen. Zanes Text in 3 und diese Fragen können dir dabei helfen.*	• What's the name of the dish? • What country does it come from? • What's in the dish? • When do you eat it? • Who cooks it? • What do you drink with it?

▶ Digital help 🔽   ▶ Wordbank 12, p. 178

al quiz 🔽 **Ich kann** mein Lieblingsgericht beschreiben. ✅

A different kind of party

1 Before you read **Look at the first picture and read sentences 1–3.** (Circle) **the right word.**

Schau dir das erste Bild an und lies die Sätze 1–3. Kreise das richtige Wort ein.

1 Lily, Zane and Sunita (are)/ aren't meeting Noah.

2 Zane is /(isn't) bringing a drink.

3 Noah and his family (are)/ aren't sitting in the park.

2.38

Lily ___ This is the park and it's 2 o'clock. But where are Noah and his family?

Zane ___ Look, there they are! Oh, and here's Sunita!

Sunita ___ Hi! What are you bringing to the party, Zane?

Zane ___ It's my special chocolate cake.

10 Lily ___ It looks really good!

Zane ___ Happy birthday, Noah! Here's a cake for you!

Noah ___ Thanks!

Lily ___ And here are some strawberries, Noah.

15

Noah ___ Thanks, but I'm allergic to strawberries, remember?

Lily ___ Oh no, I'm sorry ...

Dad ___ That's OK, Lily. I love strawberries!

20

2.39

Sunita		Zane, are you OK? You're very quiet.
Zane		Erm, we're just[1] sitting and talking. There's no music, no dancing … It's not the kind of party I like!
25 **Sunita**		But Noah doesn't like loud music or dancing. So I think this is the kind of party he likes.

Dad		Do you want to open your presents now, Noah?
30 **Noah**		No, let's eat my birthday trifle first!
Dad		OK, it's in my bag over there … Oh no! Stop, Buddy!
Noah		Is Buddy OK?
Mum		Yes, he's OK. But we can't eat it now!
35		I'm sorry, Noah.
Noah		That's no problem. We can eat Zane's chocolate cake.

Noah		This is the best birthday party ever[2]! I'm having a picnic with my family and my best friends and my dog. It isn't too loud, so I'm feeling good. It's sunny, I have presents and chocolate cake. It's the perfect party for me!
Lily		That's great!

45 **Noah**		And now – my secret: Watch this!
Sunita		Wow! Noah, that's great!
Zane		You're really good at juggling!
Noah		Ta-dah! This is a circus birthday party, right?
50 **Zane**		Wow, this is a great party! Thanks, Noah!

---

[1] **just** *nur, bloß*   [2] **the best birthday party ever** *die beste Party überhaupt*

2 Who is it?

Circle the right name. *Kreise den richtigen Namen ein.*

1 **Zane** / Lily brings a chocolate cake to the party.

2 Noah / **Lily** brings strawberries to the party.

3 **Noah** / Zane can't eat strawberries.

4 Lily / **Buddy** eats the birthday trifle.

3 Words in the story

Find the English words 1–4 in the story and write them.
Finde die Wörter 1–4 in Englisch in der Story und schreibe sie auf.

1 besonders *(line 8)* *special* 2 Geschenke *(line 28)* *presents*

3 Geheimnis *(line 46)* *secret* 4 jonglieren *(line 48)* *juggling*

4 Life skills **People are different**

a) **Tick (✓) the box next to the sentence that is true for you.**
Mache ein Häkchen (✓) in das Kästchen hinter jedem Satz, der auf dich zutrifft.

1 I like quiet parties.	☐	I don't like quiet parties.	☐
2 I like loud music.	☐	I don't like loud music.	☐
3 I love strawberries.	☐	I don't love strawberries.	☐
4 I eat meat.	☐	I don't eat meat.	☐

b) **Talk to your partner. What's the same and what's different?**
Sprich mit deinem Partner oder deiner Partnerin. Was ist gleich und was ist anders?

I don't eat pork[1]. What about you?

I eat pork, so that's different. I like skateboarding.

Cool! I like skateboarding too. That's the same.

[1] **pork** *Schweinefleisch*

Digital quiz 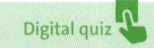 **Ich kann** über Unterschiede sprechen.

The Brighton dares: A birthday

1 Birthday words

Before you watch ~~Cross out~~ the two words that are not **birthday** words. *Streiche die beiden Wörter durch, die keine Geburtstagswörter sind.*

1 cake	2 party	3 ~~vet~~	4 singing
5 games	6 music	7 dancing	8 ~~window~~

2 Viewing **The party**

a) **Watch parts 1–4. Complete Gloria's birthday invitation.** *Schau dir die Teile 1–4 an. Ergänze Glorias Geburtstagseinladung.*

PLEASE COME TO MY PARTY!

On *Saturday* 11th at *6* o'clock

for party games and *music*

Gloria

b) **Watch parts 5–8. Circle the correct words.** *Schau dir die Teile 5–8 an. Kreise die richtigen Wörter ein.*

1 Emir does his dare[1] at the party / (supermarket).
2 Daisy makes a video of Emir. He is dancing / (singing).
3 The people in the supermarket are (happy) / angry.
4 The toy[2] dog is a birthday present from Daisy / (Sota).

c) **Watch the last two parts. Answer the question.** *Schau dir die letzten beiden Teile an. Beantworte die Frage.*

What are the friends doing when the video finishes[3]? They are *dancing* .

3 All the dares

There are ten dares in this book. Which is the best dare? *Es gibt zehn Mutproben in diesem Buch. Welche ist die beste Wette?*

I think	Daisy's Emir's	school family sports and hobbies town birthday	dare is	the best. cool. funny. mean. weird.

---

[1] **dare** *Mutprobe* [2] **toy** *Spielzeug* [3] **finish** *enden*

Explaining words

1 Use umbrella words

a) **Write the food and drinks under the correct umbrella word. Check in the Wordbank on page 178 if you're not sure.** *Schreibe die Lebensmittel und Getränke unter den richtigen Oberbegriff. Schau in der Wordbank auf Seite 178 nach, wenn du nicht sicher bist.*

chicken • melon • milk • pepper • spaghetti

☂ pasta	☂ meat	☂ drink	☂ fruit	☂ vegetable
spaghetti	*chicken*	*milk*	*melon*	*pepper*
noodles	*sausage*	*lemonade*	*lemon*	*carrot*

▶ Wordbank 12, p. 178

b) **Now write these words under the correct umbrella word.** *Nun trage diese Wörter unter dem richtigen Oberbegriff ein.*

carrot • sausage • lemon • noodles • lemonade

Chips are a kind of potato. Potatoes are a kind of vegetable. Vegetables are good for you. So chips are good for you, right?

2 Describe it

Write three words from the box that describe each food or drink. *Schreibe zu jedem Lebensmittel oder Getränk drei Wörter aus der Box, die es beschreiben.*

black • drink • green • hot • long • orange • small • sweet • vegetable

1 cola: *black, sweet, drink*

2 carrot: *orange, long, vegetable*

3 tea: *hot, green/black, drink*

4 peas: *small, green, vegetable*

3 Game **Explain it!**

Bildet Dreiergruppen. Jedes Kind schreibt zwei Wörter (Essen und Getränke) auf je einen Zettel. Tauscht die Zettel mit einer anderen Gruppe, aber schaut euch die neuen Zettel noch nicht an. In jeder Gruppe nimmt ein Kind einen Zettel und erklärt den anderen das Wort. Die anderen müssen raten.

It's small and red. It's a fruit.   Strawberry?   Yes!

Digital quiz 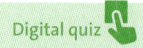   **Ich kann Wörter erklären.** ✓

Make a class recipe book

Step 1: Plan your recipe

Choose a dish.

You can use your favourite dish from page 151.

Write a shopping list.

Wähle ein Gericht aus.

Du kannst dein Lieblingsessen von Seite 151 nehmen. Schreibe eine Einkaufsliste.

▶ Wordbank 12, p. 178

Pancakes with lemon and sugar

You need: 2 eggs
300g flour
1 litre milk
50g butter
salt
lemons
sugar

Step 2: Write about your dish

You can use your text from page 151.

Du kannst deinen Text von Seite 151 nutzen.

I like …

This dish is from …

You make it / them with …

I eat it / them with …

It's / They're great!

▶ Wordbank 13, p. 179

I like pancakes.
I eat them with lemon and sugar.

Step 3: Decorate your page

Use photos or draw pictures of your dish. *Verwendet Fotos oder malt ein Bild von eurem Gericht.*

They're great!

Step 4: Give feedback

Collect all the recipes.

Read them and write feedback.

Sammelt alle Rezepte ein.

Lest sie und schreibt ein Feedback.

This is a good recipe!

I want to make this!

1 A film night

 Ich kann **über Essen sprechen.**

a) Words   Write the missing letters. Check in the vocabulary list if you're not sure.
Schreibe die fehlenden Buchstaben auf. Schau im Vocabulary nach, wenn du nicht sicher bist.

1   c _a_ r _ro_ t s

2   s _t_ r _a_ w b e r r i e s

3   t _o_ m _a_ t _o_ e s

4   b _re_ a d

5   s _a_ u _s_ a _g_ e _s_

6   c h _o_ c _o_ l a _t_ e

7   m _i_ l _k_

8   l _e_ m _o_ n _a_ d _e_

b)   You are having a film night. What do you want to buy? Choose three things. *Du planst einen Filmabend. Was möchtest du dafür einkaufen? Wähle drei Dinge aus.*

2   Language   After the party

Look at the picture and complete the sentences with the words in the box.
Schau dir das Bild an und ergänze die Sätze mit Wörtern aus der Box.

> *How much food and drink is there?*

| a lot of • aren't • carrots • isn't • sausages |

1   There _isn't_ much lemonade.

2   There _aren't_ many sandwiches.

3   There's _a lot of_ salad.

4   There are a lot of _sausages_ .

5   There aren't many _carrots_ .

 Check

2.40
3 Listening **Dinner at Sunita's house**

a) **Zane is at Sunita's house for dinner. Listen. Tick (✓) the correct picture.** *Zane ist zum Abendessen bei Sunita. Höre zu. Mache ein Häkchen (✓) an das richtige Bild.*

b) **Listen again. Draw lines.** *Höre noch einmal zu. Ziehe Verbindungslinien.*

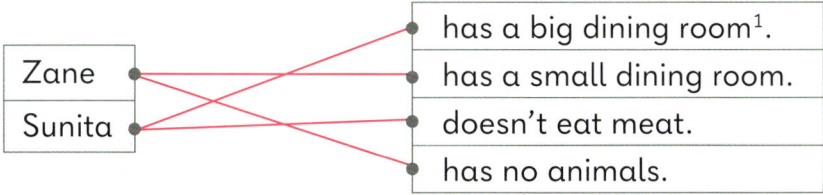

Zane · ─── · has a big dining room[1].
Sunita · ─── · has a small dining room.
· doesn't eat meat.
· has no animals.

---

4 Study skills **Explaining new words**

One word in each sentence is wrong. Write the correct word from the box.
Ein Wort in jedem Satz ist falsch. Finde das richtige in der Box und schreibe es auf.

after • drink • good • hot • meat • milk • ~~vegetable~~

1 carrot: It's a ~~drink~~ *vegetable* _____.

2 chicken: It's ~~fruit~~ *meat* _____.

3 trifle: You eat it ~~before~~ *after* _____ dinner.

4 milk: It's a kind of ~~food~~ *drink* _____.

5 **cornflakes**: You eat them with ~~lemonade~~ *milk* _____.

6 tea: It's a ~~cold~~ *hot* _____ drink.

7 vegetables: They're ~~bad~~ *good* _____ for you.

---

[1] **dining room** *Esszimmer*

Check

👥 10   Speaking **Find the differences** ▶ p. 145

Partner B: Sieh dir das Bild an. Beschreibe von 1–6, was du siehst. Wechsel dich mit Partner/in A ab. Findet sechs Unterschiede.

> taking a photo • talking •
> looking at a girl • drawing •
> eating popcorn • eating apples

Number 1: In my picture a boy and a girl are singing.

In my picture they are talking. Number 2: …

11   **My party photos** ▶ p. 145

A

B

C

D

Extra practice 1 ▶ page 142

Sunita and Ryan write to Noah. Put their messages in the right order.

Sunita und Ryan schreiben Noah. Ordne ihre Nachrichten in der richtigen Reihenfolge.

2   I'd love to come to your party. Thanks.

1   Hi, Noah

3   See you in the park on Saturday.

4   Love Sunita

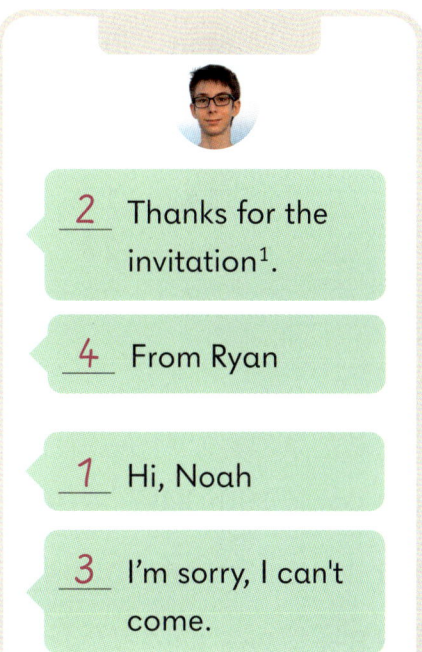

2   Thanks for the invitation[1].

4   From Ryan

1   Hi, Noah

3   I'm sorry, I can't come.

Extra practice 2 ▶ page 142

🔊 2.28

Listen and read. *Höre zu und lese.*

Thirty days have September
April, June and November
All the rest[2] have 31
February's great with 28
And a leap year's[3] fine with 29!

1   Colour the months with 30 days in green.

2   Colour the months with 31 days in yellow.

3   Colour the month with 28 or 29 days in blue.

January *(gelb)*
February *(blau)*
March *(gelb)*
April *(grün)*
May *(gelb)*
June *(grün)*
July *(gelb)*
August *(gelb)*
September *(grün)*
October *(gelb)*
November *(grün)*
December *(gelb)*

[1] **invitation** *Einladung* [2] **rest** *Rest* [3] **leap year** *Schaltjahr*

Extra practice 3 ▶ page 143

Look at the calendar and answer the questions.
Sieh dir den Kalender an und beantworte die Fragen.

JULY

Mon	Tue	Wed	Thu	Fri	Sat	Sun
	1	2	3	4	5	6
7	8	9	10	11	12	13
14	15	16	17	18	19	20
21	22	23	24	25	26	27
28	29	30	31			

1 What day is 3rd July? *Thursday*

2 What day is 19th July? *Saturday*

3 What day is 13th July? *Sunday*

4 What day is 2nd July? *Wednesday*

Extra practice 4 ▶ page 145

2.31

Listen to the sounds. Write 2–6. *Höre dir die Geräusche an. Schreibe 2–6.*

1 They are drinking tea.

2 She is writing a message.

3 They are playing table tennis.

4 He's eating toast.

5 She's closing[1] the car door.

6 He's boxing.

---
[1] **close** *schließen*

▶ page 145

Extra practice 5

Look at the pictures. What are the people doing? Complete the sentences with the words in the box. *Sieh dir die Bilder an. Was machen die Personen? Ergänze die Sätze mit den Wörtern in der Box.*

| is going • are making • is sleeping¹ • is getting up • are eating |

The girl in Mexico *is sleeping*_____.

The boy in New York *is getting up*____.

In London they *are making*_____ lunch.

In Tokyo they *are eating*_____ dinner.

In Sydney they *are going*_____ to bed.

¹ **sleep** *schlafen*

▶ page 148

Extra practice 6

a) **Zane wants to cook dinner. He has a lot of questions. Complete the questions with** *much* **or** *many*. *Zane möchte kochen. Er hat viele Fragen. Ergänze seine Fragen mit* much *oder* many.

How <u>many</u> tomatoes do we need?

And how <u>much</u> meat?

And how <u>many</u> carrots?

How <u>much</u> cheese do I need for the pasta?

And how <u>much</u> pasta do we need?

b) **Look at the blue words in a). What dish does Zane want to cook? Tick (✓) the right picture.** *Sieh dir die blauen Wörter in a) an. Was möchte Zane kochen? Hake (✓) das richtige Bild ab.*

A ☐   B ☐   C ✓

c) **Zane is in the kitchen. Look at the picture and read the sentences. Tick (✓) the true sentences.** *Zane ist in der Küche. Sieh dir das Bild an und lies die Sätze. Hake (✓) die richtigen Sätze ab.*

1 There are a lot of tomatoes. ✓

2 There isn't much meat. ✓

3 There are a lot of carrots. ☐

4 There is a lot of pasta. ☐

🔊 Unit 5 – Enjoy!

pp. 140/141

food	das Essen
trifle	das Trifle *(britischer Nachtisch)*
fruit	das Obst
cream	die Sahne
strawberry	die Erdbeere
allergic (to)	allergisch (gegen)
meat	das Fleisch
Indian	indisch; der Inder, die Inderin
cheese	der Käse
pea	die Erbse
tomato, *pl* **tomatoes**	die Tomate
bread	das Brot
rice	der Reis
vegetables *(pl)*	das Gemüse

strawberries and **cream**.

peas

tomato sauce
(die Tomatensoße)

tomato

Topic 1

▶ p. 142

cake	der Kuchen, die Torte
(to) come	(mit)kommen
May	der Mai

The months (die Monate)

1 January der Januar	**4 April** der April	**7 July** der Juli
2 February der Februar	**5 May** der Mai	**8 August** der August
3 March der März	**6 June** der Juni	**9 September** der September

10 October der Oktober
11 November der November
12 December der Dezember

circus	der Zirkus

▶ p. 143 **the first of April (1st April)**   der erste April

1st **first** erste(r,s)	**2nd** **second** zweite(r,s)	**3rd** **third** dritte(r,s)	**4th** **fourth** vierte(r,s)	**5th** **fifth** fünfte(r,s)	**8th** **eighth** achter(r,s)	**9th** **ninth** neunter(r,s)	**12th** **twelfth** zwölfte(r,s)

▶ Numbers, p. 168

▶ p. 144

(to) juggle	jonglieren

▶ p. 145

(to) sit	sitzen; sich setzen
picture	das Bild
number	die Zahl, die Nummer

in the picture = auf dem Bild

Topic 2

▶ p.146	(to) **need** sth.	etwas brauchen
	present	das Geschenk
	magic set	der Zauberkasten
	light	das Licht; die Lampe
	perfect	perfekt
▶ p.147	salad	der Salat *(als Gericht oder Beilage)*
	carrot	die Möhre, die Karotte
	melon	die Melone
	lemonade	die Limonade
	packet	die Packung, das Päckchen
	sausage	das (Brat-, Bock-)Würstchen, die Wurst
	lemon	die Zitrone
	sugar	der Zucker
	already	schon
	shopping list	die Einkaufsliste

a **present**

lemons

Topic 3

▶ p.150	butter	die Butter
	cocoa	der Kakao
	egg	das Ei
	flour	das Mehl
	icing	die Glasur, der Zuckerguss
	milk	die Milch
	oil	das Öl
	salt	das Salz
	mixture	die Mischung
	(to) add	hinzufügen, addieren
▶ p.151	dish	das Gericht *(die Mahlzeit)*
	onion	die Zwiebel
	pepper	die Paprika, die Peperoni; der Pfeffer
	chicken	das Huhn; das (Brat-)Hähnchen
	kind (of)	die Art (von), die Sorte (von)
	banana	die Banane
	every	jede(r, s)
	(to) drink	trinken

eggs, milk, flour, sugar

(to) **mix** = (ver)mischen, mixen

an **onion**

a **drink** = ein Getränk

Story

Study skills

Unit task

🔊 English numbers

1	one		1st	first	
2	two		2nd	second	
3	three		3rd	third	
4	four		4th	fourth	
5	five		5th	fifth	
6	six		6th	sixth	
7	seven		7th	seventh	
8	eight		8th	eighth	
9	nine		9th	ninth	
10	ten		10th	tenth	
11	eleven		11th	eleventh	
12	twelve		12th	twelfth	
13	thirteen		13th	thirteenth	
14	fourteen		14th	fourteenth	
15	fifteen		15th	fifteenth	
16	sixteen		16th	sixteenth	
17	seventeen		17th	seventeenth	
18	eighteen		18th	eighteenth	
19	nineteen		19th	nineteenth	
20	twenty		20th	twentieth	
21	twenty-one		21st	twenty-first	
22	twenty-two		22nd	twenty-second	
23	twenty-three		23rd	twenty-third	
24	twenty-four		24th	twenty-fourth	
25	twenty-five		25th	twenty-fifth	
26	twenty-six		26th	twenty-sixth	
27	twenty-seven		27th	twenty-seventh	
28	twenty-eight		28th	twenty-eighth	
29	twenty-nine		29th	twenty-ninth	
30	thirty		30th	thirtieth	
31	thirty-one		31st	thirty-first	

Wordbank 1: Numbers

▶ Hello!, p. 10

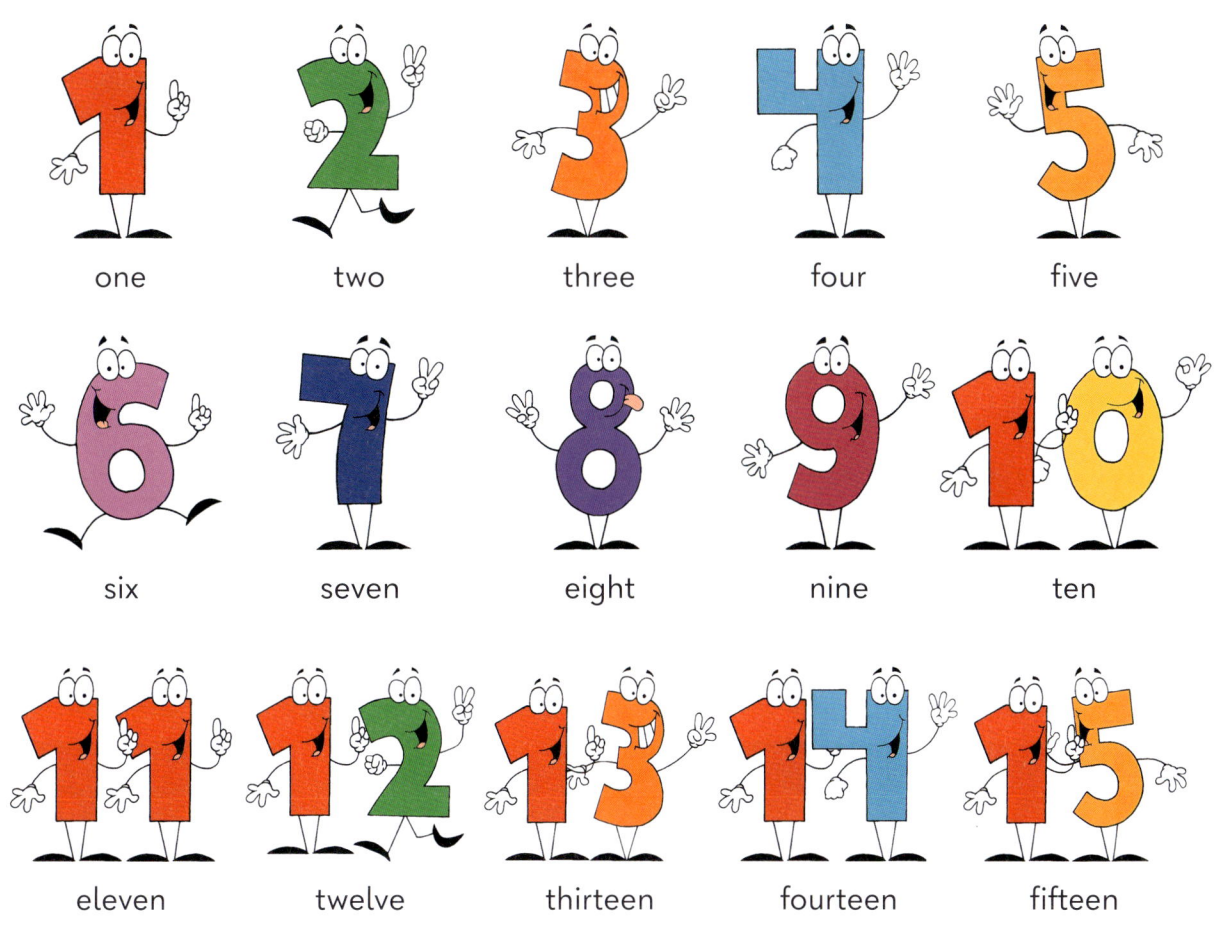

one   two   three   four   five

six   seven   eight   nine   ten

eleven   twelve   thirteen   fourteen   fifteen

Wordbank 2: Colours

▶ Hello!, p. 12

orange • purple • red • yellow • green • blue • brown • black • white

Wordbank 3: Animals

▶ Hello!, p. 14

cat, dog, elephant, fish, horse, lion, monkey, parrot, seagull, snake, ...

a bear

a butterfly

a crocodile

a dolphin

a duck

a llama

a meerkat[1]

My favourite animal is ...

an owl

a panda

a penguin

a rhino

a spider

a tiger

a whale

[1] **meerkat** *Erdmännchen*

Wordbank 4: Free time

► Hello!, p. 15

dancing, drawing, football, listening to music, taking photos, swimming, ...

baking

basketball

boxing

climbing

coding

cycling

nail art

My favourite hobby is ...
My favourite sport is ...
I like ...
I love ...
I don't like ...

gaming

gymnastics

hanging out with friends

judo

kayaking

horse riding

reading

Wordbank 5: School subjects

▶ Unit 1, p. 27

art, computing, design and technology, English, French, maths, music, PE, …

German (*Deutsch*)

media studies (*Medienkompetenz*)

school club (*AG*)

business and employment studies: technology, economics, home economics (*Arbeitslehre: Technik, Wirtschaft, Hauswirtschaft*)

science: biology, chemistry, physics (*Naturwissenschaften: Biologie, Chemie, Physik*)

social studies: history, geography, politics (*Gesellschaftswissenschaften: Geschichte, Geografie, Politik*)

ethics (*Ethik*)

RE religious education (*Religionslehre*)

philosophy (*Philosophie*)

special needs support (*Förderunterricht*)

study time (*Arbeitsstunde, Eigenarbeit, Hausaufgaben*)

tutor time (*Klassenlehrerstunde/ Verfügungsstunde*)

Wordbank 6: Places at school

▶ Unit 1, p. 29

art room, canteen, classroom, computer room, corridor, sports hall, ...

cinema

dance studio

drama room

games room

library

music room

office

playground

science lab

sports field

staff room

swimming pool

Wordbank 7: Family

▶ Unit 2, p. 49

parents / grandparents	die Eltern / die Großeltern
child / children	das Kind / die Kinder
son / daughter	der Sohn / die Tochter
grandson / granddaughter	der Enkel / die Enkelin
blended family	die Patchworkfamilie
separated	getrennt
husband / wife	der Ehemann / die Ehefrau
single	alleinstehend
niece / nephew	Nichte / Neffe

Wordbank 8: Pets

▶ Unit 2, p. 53

cat, dog, fish, hamster, horse, parrot, rabbit, snake

budgie *(der Wellensittich)*

chicken *(das Huhn)*

ferret *(das Frettchen)*

guinea pig *(das Meer- schweinchen)*

kitten *(das Kätzchen)*

lizard *(die Echse)*

mouse *(die Maus)*

puppy *(der Welpe)*

rabbit *(das Kaninchen)*

rat *(die Ratte)*

Wordbank 9: Things in my room

▶ Unit 2, p. 55

disco ball

curtains

loft bed

blind

fairy lights

plant

closet

screen

carpet

games console

beanbag

hammock

Wordbank 10: The times of the day

▶ Unit 3, p. 82

DAY

in the morning
at 7 o'clock
at 7 a.m.

at noon

in the afternoon
at 4 o'clock
at 4 p.m.

NIGHT

in the evening
at 7 o'clock
at 7 p.m.

at night
at 3 o'clock
at 3 a.m.

at night
at 11 o'clock
at 11 p.m.

at midnight

Wordbank 11: Places in my town or village

▶ Unit 4, p. 117

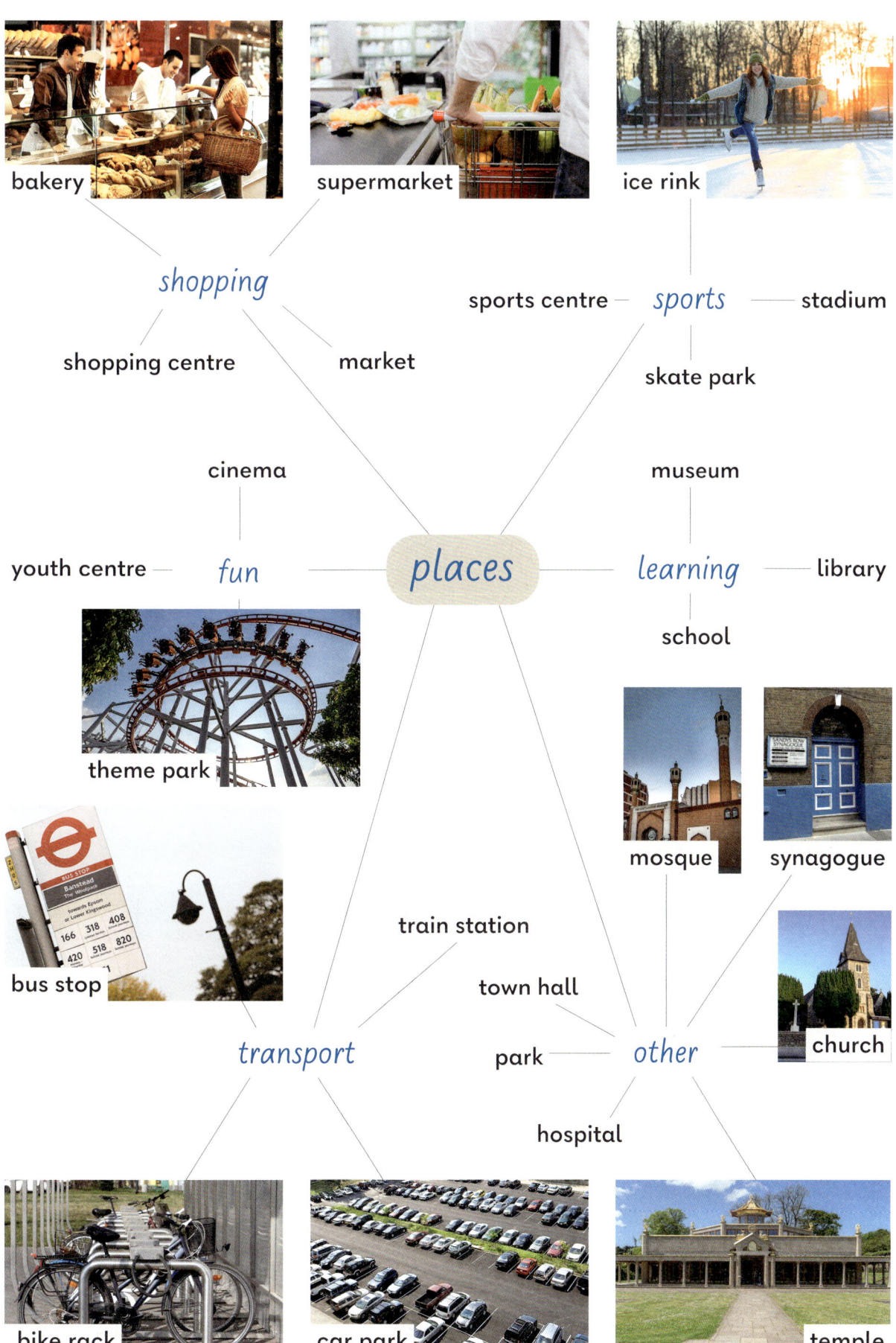

bakery

supermarket

ice rink

shopping

shopping centre

market

sports centre — *sports* — stadium

skate park

cinema

museum

youth centre — *fun*

places

learning — library

school

theme park

mosque

synagogue

bus stop

train station

town hall

church

transport

park — *other*

hospital

bike rack

car park

temple

Wordbank 12: Food

▶ Unit 5, p. 149

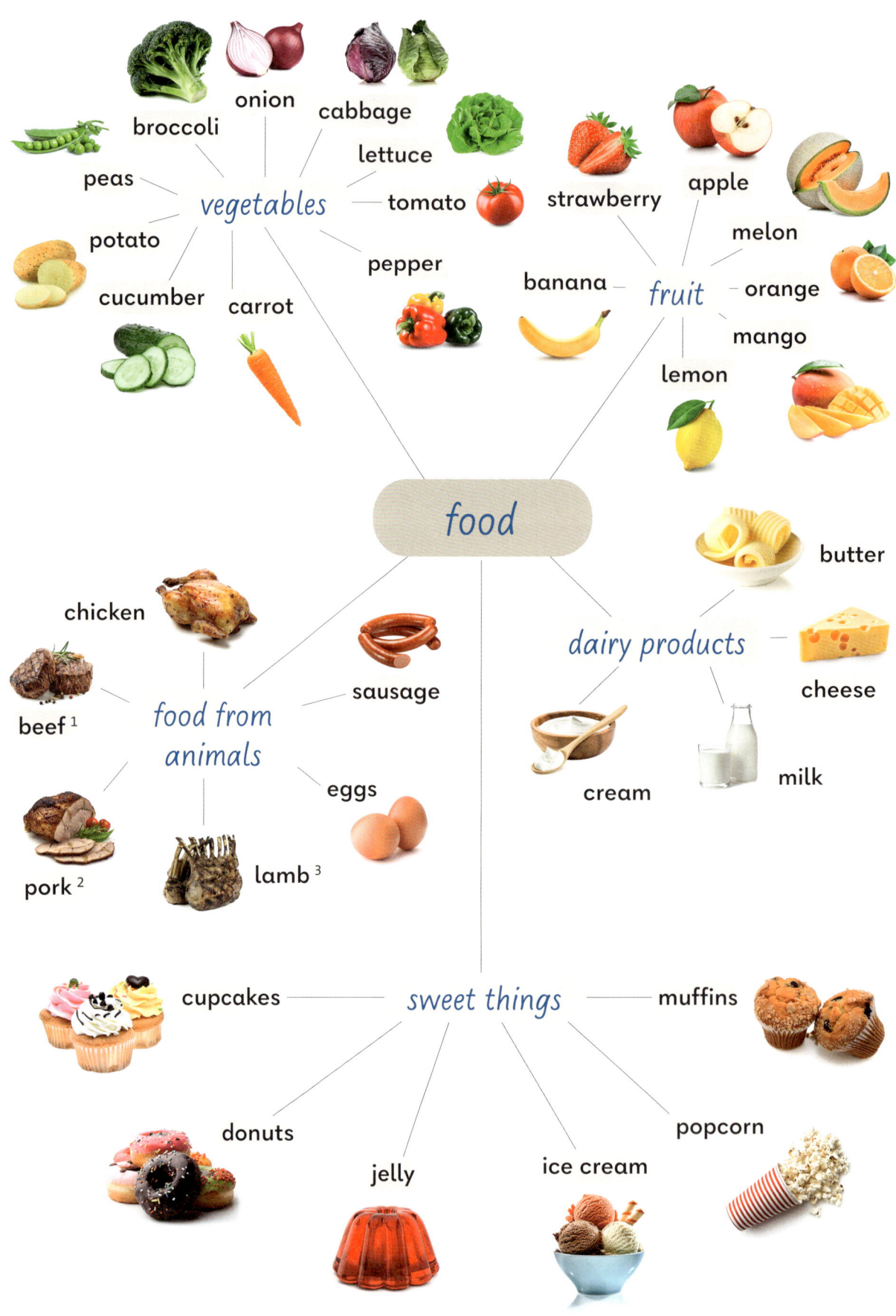

vegetables

broccoli

onion

cabbage

lettuce

peas

potato

cucumber

carrot

tomato

pepper

strawberry

apple

melon

banana

fruit

orange

mango

lemon

food

butter

dairy products

cheese

chicken

beef [1]

sausage

food from animals

eggs

cream

milk

pork [2]

lamb [3]

cupcakes

sweet things

muffins

donuts

jelly

ice cream

popcorn

---

[1] **beef** *Rindfleisch*   [2] **pork** *Schweinefleisch*   [2] **lamb** *Lamm; Lammfleisch*

Wordbank 13: Cooking

▸ Unit 5, p. 157

(to) add

(to) bake

(to) boil

(to) cut

(to) fry

(to) mix

(to) pour

(to) roll out

(to) stir

baking tray

frying pan

oven

saucepan

spoon

whisk

Titelbild
Cornelsen/Personen: Anja Poehlmann, Brighton Pier: mauritius images/Steve Vidler

Umschlagseiten
Vorne: Miniaturseiten im Umschlag und S. 1: Bitte siehe unter der jeweiligen Seitenzahl;
Hinten: Karte: stock.adobe.com/lesniewski, Möwe: Irina Zinner

Illustrationen
Cornelsen/**Harald Ardeias**: (S. 4 Mann; S. 5 Topic 2 + Story; S. 6 Topic 2, Topic 3 +Story; S. 7 Topic 1+Story; S. 8 Topic 2+Story; S. 9 Topic 2+Story; S. 17: oben + Mitte je 1-5 (2; S.21 oben; S. 22 oben; S. 26; S. 27 oben + mi.re.; S. 29 mi.; S. 30; S. 31; S. 33 (A, B, C); S. 36 mi.; S. 37; S. 38; S. 41 unten; S. 42/1-4; S. 50 oben; S. 55 mitte re., S. 56; S. 57 oben; S. 58 mitte re., S. 60; S. 61; S. 63 family tree; S. 66 oben re.; S. 67 oben; S. 74–76; S. 82 oben re.; S. 84 mitte re.; S. 91 unten re.; S. 92-93; S. 95 mitte; S. 99/1-5; S. 100/1-5; S. 102 unten re.; S. 117-118; S. 120/A-E; S. 122 unten; S. 123; S. 129; S. 132 oben li.; S. 135; S. 143 mitte re.; S. 144 oben re.; S. 145 oben re.+mitte re.; S. 146 mitte; S. 147 oben re.; S. 148; S. 151 oben li.; S. 152-154; S. 158 unten re.; S. 159; S. 160 oben re.; S. 163/1-5; S. 174; S. 175 unten). Cornelsen/Inhouse/**Josephine Bienert-Köhler**: (S. 5 Unit task; S. 6 Unit task; S. 35; S. 59 My room; S. 65 My dream room; S. 157 Pan-cakes). Cornelsen/**Karen Donnelly** (S. 5 Topic 1+Study skills; S. 17: 6; S. 23 unten; S. 25: A-D; S.34; S. 39; S. 69/1-6; S. 81 unten; S. 85/A-E; S. 100 oben; S. 104; S. 112 oben li.; S. 162: 1-6; S. 164 unten re.). Cornelsen/**Irina Zinner**: (S. 4 obere drei Bilder; S. 6 Möwen; S. 9 Möwen; S. 10; S. 11; S. 12 oben; S. 13; S. 14 unten re.; S. 15: 1-4 + unten re.; S. 16 mi.re.; S. 17 Möwen; S. 18 Möwe; S. 23 Möwe; S. 27 Möwen; S. 29 Möwe; S. 32 Möwe; S. 43 Möwe; S. 50 mitte re.; S. 51 Möwe; S. 53 Möwe; S. 55 Möwe; S. 58 (A-F); S. 59 Möwe; S. 64 Möwe; S. 65 Möwe; S. 72 Möwe; S. 84 Möwe; S. 85 Möwe; S. 87 unten; S. 89 Möwe; S. 91 Möwe; S. 94 Möwe; S. 97 Möwe; S. 103; S. 110 Möwe; S. 113 Möwe; S. 115; S. 119 Möwe; S. 121 Möwe; S. 124 Möwe; S. 127 Möwe; S. 143 Möwen; S. 144 Möwe; S. 145 Möwe; S. 149 Möwe; S. 151 Möwe; S. 156 Möwe, S.157 Möwe; S. 184).

Abbildungen
S. 5 My new school+Topic 3: Cornelsen/Anja Poehlmann; **S. 6** My family and home: Cornelsen/Anja Poehlmann; **S. 7** My day+Topic 3: Cornelsen/Anja Poehlmann, Topic 2: Shutterstock.com/Daisy Daisy, Study skills: Shutterstock.com/CroMary, Unit task: Shutterstock.com/Pereslavtseva Katerina; **S. 8** Where I live: mauritius images/alamy stock photo/Chris Harris, Topic 1: mauritius images/alamy stock photo/Nigel Bowles, Topic 3: mauritius images/alamy stock photo/Eye Ubiquitous, Study skills: Shutterstock.com/Nataliya Dorokhina, Unit task: Shutterstock.com/BearFotos; **S. 9** Enjoy: Shutterstock.com/CKP1001, Topic 3: stock.adobe.com/uckyo; **S. 12** unten li. Shutterstock.com/Pete Pahham, unten mi. Shutterstock.com/New Africa; unten re. Shutterstock.com/Djomas; **S. 14:** 1 stock.adobe.com/Arija, 2 Panther Media GmbH/Gertrud Böttcher, 3 Shutterstock.com/Dmitrijs Mihejevs, 4 Shutterstock.com/Iakov Filimonov, 5 Shutterstock.com/Eric Isselee, 6 Shutterstock.com/Alex Staroseltsev, 7 Shutterstock.com/bluedog studio, 8 Shutterstock.com/Susan Schmitz; **S. 15** mi. Shutterstock.com/Yefym Turkin; **S. 16** oben li. Shutterstock.com/Eric Isselee; **S. 18** 1+2: Cornelsen/Anja Poehlmann; **S. 19** 3+4: Cornelsen/Anja Poehlmann; **S. 20** oben: Cornelsen/Anja Poehlmann, unten li: Shutterstock.com/AnnaStills, unten re.: Shutterstock.com/p_ponomareva; **S. 21** unten: Shutterstock.com/Monkey Business Images; **S. 22** Mitte: Cornelsen/Anja Poehlmann; **S. 23** Shutterstock.com/AnnaStills; **S. 24** oben re. + mi. 1+3+4: Cornelsen/Anja Poehlmann, Tabelle: Shutterstock.com/zzveillust; **S. 25** Junge: Cornelsen/Anja Poehlmann, Mädchen: Shutterstock.com/antoniodiaz; **S. 28:** 1 mauritius images/alamy stock photo/Greg Balfour Evans, 2+4 Cornelsen/Anja Poehlmann, 3 mauritius images/alamy stock photo/James Winspear-VIEW; **S. 32** unten re.: Cornelsen/Anja Poehlmann; **S. 33** oben re. (Filmstill): Grasshopper Films LTD; **S. 36** 1: Shutterstock.com/file404, 2: Shutterstock.com/Quinn Martin, 3: Shutterstock.com/Monkey Business Images, 4: Shutterstock.com/guig120; **S. 41** oben re. Cornelsen/Anja Poehlmann; **S. 44** Elefant, Schlange: Shutterstock.com/Teguh Mujiono, Fische: Shutterstock.com/Tatyana Vyc, Hütte: Shutterstock.com/MicroOne, unten re.: Shutterstock.com/Adam Gregor; **S. 45** tired: Shutterstock.com/Lapina, uniforms: Shutterstock.com/miniwide,

pen, rubber + ruler: Shutterstock.com/jottaonni; **S. 46** Shutterstock.com/EugeneEdge; **S. 48** Mira, Nish: Cornelsen/li. (Sunita): Cornelsen/Anja Poehlmann, Mitte: Shutterstock.com/insta_photos, re.: Shutterstock.com/V.S.Anandhakrishna, Ben: Shutterstock.com/Txema Gerardo, Willow: Shutterstock.com/JacquiMoore, mitte li.: Cornelsen/Anja Poehlmann, mitte re.: Shutterstock.com/StockImageFactory.com; **S. 49** Cornelsen/Anja Poehlmann; **S. 51** unten: Shutterstock.com/all_about_people; **S. 52** 1: Shutterstock.com/Joan Carles Juarez, 2: Shutterstock.com/Volodymyr Plysiuk, unten re.: Shutterstock.com/Bilal Kocabas; **S. 53** Rex: Shutterstock.com/Ga_photo, Axel: Shutterstock.com/FlavoredPixels, Maude: Shutterstock.com/D.Bond, Lily: Cornelsen/Anja Poehlmann; **S. 54** 1: mauritius images/alamy stock photo/Natalie Jezzard, 2: mauritius images/Novarc Images, 3: mauritius images/alamy stock photo/Edward Simons, 4: mauritius images/alamy stock photo/Paul Thompson Images; **S. 55** Lily: Cornelsen/Anja Poehlmann; **S. 57** Sunita: Cornelsen/Anja Poehlmann; **S. 62** guitar: Shutterstock.com/Mircea Pavel, dinner: Shutterstock.com/Aleksandra Duda, messages: Shutterstock.com/Reservoir Dots, game: Shutterstock.com/Net Vector, headphones: Shutterstock.com/maximmmmum, cook: Shutterstock.com/michaeljung; **S. 63** oben re.+unten 1-4 (Filmstills): Cornelsen/Grasshopper Films, hug: Shutterstock.com/AKalenskyi, postbox: stock.adobe.com/lineartestpilot, clock: stock.adobe.com/SKphotographer; **S. 66** Mrs Taylor: Shutterstock.com/Nenad Aksic, Lily: Cornelsen/Anja Poehlmann; **S. 67** hamster: Shutterstock.com/Johannes Menge, parrot: Shutterstock.com/HRP_Photography; **S. 68** dog: stock.adobe.com/Fly_dragonfly, snake: Shutterstock.com/Robles Designery, Emoticon: Shutterstock.com/Yefym Turkin, Drago: Shutterstock.com/Moravian; **S. 69** mitte re. paperfamily: stock.adobe.com/Renat, oben doors: Shutterstock.com/Bibadash**;** **S. 70** Lyle u. Astra: stock.adobe.com/Pixel-Shot, tree: Shutterstock.com/Anterovium, stockings: stock.adobe.com/gertrudda, cookies: Shutterstock.com/Vladimir Kruglove, turkey: stock.adobe.com/Brent Hofacker; **S. 71** Vivian: stock.adobe.com/themorningglory, mitte re.: Shutterstock.com/Pichaya Pureesrisak, unten: ClipDealer GmbH/szefei; **S. 72** Silhouetten: Shutterstock.com/AlexHliv; **S. 73** 1: Shutterstock.com/oksana2010, 2: Shutterstock.com/Eric Isselee, 3: Shutterstock.com/Donovan van Staden, 4: Shutterstock.com/PetlinDmitry; **S. 77**: vet: Shutterstock.com/Noi1990, garden: Shutterstock.com/brgfx; **S. 78**: chair: Shutterstock.com/photka; **S. 80** A+B: Cornelsen/Anja Poehlmann, Emoticon: Shutterstock.com/Yefym Turkin, heart: Shutterstock.com/pink.mousy, unten re.: Shutterstock.com/Panuwach; **S. 81** C+D: Cornelsen/Anja Poehlmann, E: Cornelsen/Mädchen: Anja Poehlmann, Hintergrund: mauritius images/alamy stock photo/PDMPhotos; **S. 83** mitte re.: Cornelsen/Frau und Hintergrund (M): Shutterstock.com/Michaelpuche, Junge (M): Anja Poehlmann; **S. 84** unten re.: Shutterstock.com/Syda Productions; **S. 85** unten re.: Cornelsen/Anja Poehlmann; **S. 86** 1: Shutterstock.com/CHARAN RATTANASUPPHASIRI, 2: Shutterstock.com/wavebreakmedia, 3: Shutterstock.com/BearFotos, 4: Shutterstock.com/SpeedKingz, 5: Shutterstock.com/Manny DaCunha, 6: Shutterstock.com/YanLev, 7: Shutterstock.com/mariakray, 8: Shutterstock.com/sakkmesterke, unten re.: Shutterstock.com/oneinchpunch; **S. 88** mitte li.ob.: Shutterstock.com/Ten03, mitte li.: Shutterstock.com/Brian McEntire, unten li.: Shutterstock.com/TunedIn by Westend61; **S. 89** oben re.: Shutterstock.com/Pressmaster, unten re.: Shutterstock.com/Daisy Daisy; **S. 90** unten re.: Cornelsen/Anja Poehlmann, Emoticons: Shutterstock.com/Yefym Turkin; **S. 94** Emoticons: Shutterstock.com/Yefym Turkin; **S. 95** oben re.: Cornelsen/Grasshopper Films; **S. 96** A: Shutterstock.com/Igor Zvencom, B: Shutterstock.com/LightField Studios, C: Shutterstock.com/CroMary, D: Shutterstock.com/Fotokostic; **S. 97** unten li.: Shutterstock.com/Elena Yakusheva, unten re.: Shutterstock.com/Pereslavtseva Katerina; **S. 98** Emoticons: Shutterstock.com/Yefym Turkin, Daumen mitte: Shutterstock.com/Cosmic_Design, unten li.: Shutterstock.com/Asier Romero, unten re.: Shutterstock.com/Panuwach, Daumen unten re.: Shutterstock.com/Azizunnahar Sadeq; **S. 107** Uhr: Shutterstock.com/Gemenacom, Dusche: Shutterstock.com/Sashkin; **S. 108** mitte re.: Shutterstock.com/Ljupco Smokovski; **S. 109** mitte re.: Shutterstock.com/pjcross; **S. 110** mitte li.: Shutterstock.com/Gill Copeland, mitte re.: mauritius images/alamy stock photo/Simon Dack News, mitte re. un.: mauritius images/alamy stock photo/Chris Harris; **S. 111** oben li.: Cornelsen/Grasshopper Films, oben re.: mauritius images/alamy stock photo/Peter Moulton, mitte li.: mauritius images/alamy stock photo/Life's Like That, mitte re.: Shutterstock.com/Marius_Comanescu; **S. 112** oben re.: Cornelsen/Mädchen: Anja Poehlmann, Fensterrahmen: Shutterstock.com/Dawid Galecki, Ausblick: mauritius images/alamy stock photo/Nigel Bowles, Ohr+Auge: stock.adobe.com/nikolae, Emoticon: Shutterstock.com/Yefym Turkin; **S. 115** Jing: Shutterstock.com/

🔊 Classroom English

Good morning! (bis 12 Uhr)	Guten Morgen!
Good afternoon! (nach 12 Uhr)	Guten Tag!
Sorry, I'm late.	Entschuldigung, dass ich zu spät komme.
Can I open / close the window, please?	Kann ich bitte das Fenster öffnen / zumachen?
Can I go to the toilet, please?	Kann ich bitte zur Toilette gehen?
Goodbye. / See you tomorrow.	Auf wiedersehen! Bis morgen.
I don't understand this exercise.	Ich verstehe die Übung nicht.
What's for homework?	Was haben wir (als Hausaufgabe) auf?
Can you help me, please?	Können Sie mir bitte helfen?
What page is it, please?	Auf welcher Seite sind wir / steht es?
What's ... in English / German?	Was heißt ... auf Englisch / Deutsch?
Can I say it in German?	Kann ich das auf Deutsch sagen?
Listen, please.	Hört bitte zu.
Open your books at page 24, please.	Schlagt bitte Seite 24 auf.
Do exercise 5 for homework, please.	Macht bitte Übung 5 als Hausaufgabe.